The Nonprofit Development Companion

The AFP Fund Development Series

The AFP Fund Development Series is intended to provide fund development professionals and volunteers, including board members (and others interested in the nonprofit sector), with top-quality publications that help advance philanthropy as voluntary action for the public good. Our goal is to provide practical, timely guidance and information on fundraising, charitable giving, and related subjects. The Association of Fundraising Professionals (AFP) and Wiley each bring to this innovative collaboration unique and important resources that result in a whole greater than the sum of its parts. For information on other books in the series, please visit:

http://www.afpnet.org

THE ASSOCIATION OF FUNDRAISING PROFESSIONALS

The Association of Fundraising Professionals (AFP) represents over 30,000 members in more than 207 chapters throughout the United States, Canada,

Mexico, and China, working to advance philanthropy through advocacy, research, education, and certification programs.

The association fosters development and growth of fundraising professionals and promotes high ethical standards in the fundraising profession. For more information or to join the world's largest association of fundraising professionals, visit www.afpnet.org.

2010-2011 AFP PUBLISHING ADVISORY COMMITTEE

CHAIR: D. C. Dreger, ACFRE
Director of Campaigns/Americas, Habitat for Humanity International
Angela Beers, CFRE
Director of Development, Devereux Pocono Center
Nina P. Berkheiser, CFRE
Principal Consultant, Your Nonprofit Advisor
Linda L. Chew, CFRE
Development Consultant
Stephanie Cory, CFRE, CAP
Director of Development, The Arc of Chester County
Patricia L. Eldred, CFRE
Director of Development, Independent Living Inc.
Samuel N. Gough, CFRE
Principal, The AFRAM Group
Larry Hostetler, CFRE
Director of Marketing and Fund Development, Sierra Vista Child & Family Services
Audrey P. Kintzi, ACFRE
Director of Development, Courage Center
Steven P. Miller, CFRE
Director of Individual Giving, American Kidney Fund
Robert J. Mueller, CFRE
Vice President, Hospice Foundation of Louisville
Maria Elena Noriega
Director, Noriega Malo & Associates
Paula K. Parrish, CFRE
Director of Advancement, Fort Worth Country Day
Michele Pearce
Director of Development, Consumer Credit Counseling Service of Greater Atlanta

The Nonprofit Development Companion

A Workbook for Fundraising Success

BRYDON M. DEWITT

WILEY

John Wiley & Sons, Inc.

Published by John Wiley & Sons, Inc., Hoboken, New Jersey.

Published simultaneously in Canada.

For general information on our other products and services or for technical support, please contact our Customer Care Department within the United States at (800) 762-2974, outside the United States at (317) 572-3993 or fax (317) 572-4002.

Wiley also publishes its books in a variety of electronic formats. Some content that appears in print may not be available in electronic books. For more information about Wiley products, visit our web site at www.wiley.com.

Library of Congress Cataloging-in-Publication Data
DeWitt, Brydon M.
    The nonprofit development companion: a workbook for fundraising success/Brydon M. DeWitt.
        p. cm. – (The AFP/Wiley fund development series; 194)
    Includes index.
        ISBN 978-0-470-58698-3; ISBN 978-0-470-90654-5 (ebk); ISBN 978-0-470-90656-9 (ebk); ISBN 978-0-470-90657-6 (ebk)
    1. Nonprofit organizations. 2. Fund raising. I. Title.
        HD62.6.D49 2010
        658.15′224—dc22

                                                                            2010016374

Printed in the United States of America.

10   9   8   7   6   5   4   3   2   1

To my wife, Lou,
who has been my partner,
my support, and my love
throughout my adult life.

Contents

Foreword

There are basic principles of nonprofit development and management. Not wishy-washy, unfocused generalizations, but clear and defined goals which, although they may vary in implementation, are nevertheless markers in a nonprofit's progression toward credibility, sustainability, and effectiveness.

Some of these include, but are by no means limited to, strategic vision and clearly defined objectives; a case for support; well-developed plans for marketing, communications, and fundraising; and staff, board, and volunteer development.

I read Brydon M. DeWitt's *The Nonprofit Development Companion* at the conclusion of the Association of Fundraising Professionals International Conference, attended by knowledgeable do-gooders, fundraisers, and other staff from a vast array of nonprofit organizations. If I had asked any of these people about the ideas included in Brydon's book, most would have said that they knew the basics discussed in this book, because the ideas in it are practically universal.

However, it is another matter indeed to find a book that lays these principles out in a straightforward and interesting way. This book does just that, with Brydon's central point clearly stated in the first chapter: "Everyone associated with your organization and everything your nonprofit does has a positive or negative impact on your ability to be successful."

Brydon spent a couple of years trying to instill that principle in me when I first came into the development field almost fifteen years ago. As a novice fundraiser for Trezevant Manor and its foundation in Memphis, Tennessee, I was paired with Brydon and learned many valuable lessons from him firsthand, while shaping the development program. Through our collaboration at that time, and through our communications in the years following, he has consistently made that central point. Brydon is, at his very core, a teacher.

There are many books available that will drill down into one particular part of development: direct mail, volunteer management, budgeting. This is not one of those books. It is not a weighty, plodding, and excessively detailed book, destined to sit on your office shelf and gather dust. It is instead a clear, concise, and comprehensive guide to managing the nonprofit development effort. It is a book to be read by nonprofit staff and passed on to board members. It keeps the big picture at the forefront of your efforts.

I plan to keep multiple copies of this book on hand for lending or giving away, knowing that the message is sound and comprehensible. It is a map for a development journey, written by one who has traveled the road many times. There are Brydon's personal stories to illustrate and make a point. There are the "must-do" stops along the way. There is something in this reading for everyone: a needed reminder for the seasoned veteran or a guidebook for one setting out for the first time. Brydon provides sensible direction and signposts along the way.

Follow this map, and you will get both where you want to go and where you need to be.

Dan Murrell
Director of Planned Giving
University of Memphis

Preface

Our country is rich with an assortment of nonprofits that address a host of societal needs. Most have begun because one entrepreneur with a caring heart and an idea engaged friends, neighbors, and relatives to understand and become involved in creating organizations to improve the human condition. Some are fortunate to have access to those with knowledge of development while a great many do not. As a result, these very worthwhile organizations have difficulty moving beyond the founding stage to growth that will enable them to fulfill their missions.

Because of an awareness and concern that a large number of valuable nonprofits do not have the budget to access development materials and training, I began writing the *Development Companion* newsletter in the fall of 1996. Each issue is topic specific—annual fund, board development, and so forth—with useable tools for chief executives, development officers, and board members to utilize in beginning or strengthening their programs to raise friends and funds. This free resource is sent by e-mail to more than 600 subscribers in several states. More recently, my firm has created the *Development Companion Online* web-based subscription service as a means to provide greater access to development resources at affordable rates.

This book is a logical progression of my commitment to delivering information and tools to as many nonprofit board members, staff members, and students of development who will choose to acquire the knowledge. The chapters are based on the fundamental parts of successful development, with appropriate examples and templates that can be adapted for each organization's needs.

This work is also meant to be a celebration of the nonprofit world and the individuals who dedicate their lives and their talents to serving others. May all of us who are fortunate to serve as nonprofit leaders and development professionals remember and appreciate the great calling that is ours.

Brydon M. DeWitt
Richmond, Virginia
October, 2010

Acknowledgments

For one who has been blessed with many friends, mentors, and colleagues, it is difficult to list but a few who have enabled the writing of this book. It is important to mention early teachers and longtime encouragers. Bob Nelson and Bob Parrish of Robert E. Nelson and Associates, Robert Stuhr, and Cal Stoney of Gonser Gerber Tinker Stuhr provided the basic knowledge of development and gave me the room to grow. Eugene Klompus, a former client and good friend, gently nagged me for years to write a book and is thrilled for that to have come to pass. Ruth Modlin Ellett and Louis Markwith, friends and colleagues of long standing, may have given me the final shove to write. Many others not listed here have also contributed in numerous ways to the creation of this work, and I thank all of them.

CHAPTER 1

How Does Development Mean?

If you have not done so before, it is time to begin thinking of development as a comprehensive concept—to move from the simple "what" understanding of the term to a more all-embracing "how". Doing otherwise can threaten your ability to move your nonprofit toward its fullest potential. Development is a process that helps an organization define itself, communicate its mission and needs, and involve its logical constituency in helping fulfill its mission and reach its potential. This concept encourages us to begin at the source of our organizational energy—the mission—and to reflect on how well our current programs, budget, staffing, and public outreach are in concert with it. Further, it causes us to review the mission statement to determine if it still meets current needs, calls us to plan and set objectives that will enable us to work toward fulfilling the mission, and requires the organizational leadership to commit to action to accomplish the objectives upon which they have agreed.

In a perfect world, using the term "development" would be an unambiguous way to define the concept and the function of the process of building a productive nonprofit organization. A large part of the problem of discussing development, however, is that we are not usually talking about the same thing. Far too many people—in the profession and out—think development is just another way to say "show me the money." This understanding and attitude about the concept of raising friends and funds gains credence through the names of our professional organizations and accreditations (e.g., Association of Fundraising Professionals, Certified Fund Raising Executive, Virginia Association of Fund-Raising Executives), in being called "fundraisers" by nonprofit board members and other volunteers, and in print in such publications as the *Chronicle of Philanthropy*. This one-dimensional view of the process and profession often inhibits the ability of development officers to build effective comprehensive development programs at their organizations.

It also leads to an inculcation of misunderstanding of the field in new development staff members. When co-chairing the Virginia Fund Raising Institute (yes,

Fund Raising) a few years ago, we decided that the overall theme for the plenary sessions should deal with the importance of marketing. Our conference title was: "Telling Your Organization's Story," and we recruited branding and marketing experts from top Virginia and national firms to deliver our main conference addresses. VFRI was a great success; however, before the conference began, we received criticism from some who were planning to attend. Their complaint? "I thought this was a fundraising conference. What's marketing got to do with it?"

DEVELOPMENT IS MARKETING

The very founding block of productive development is marketing, not sales. Each nonprofit must interpret the organization and its funding needs to its identified constituents in ways that help them understand how their needs are met by being engaged with the nonprofit, both with their time and their money.

Many years ago, Phillip Kotler, professor of marketing at Northwestern University, wondered if there were similarities between marketing in the for-profit and the nonprofit worlds. Through his research, he discovered that they were mainly the same and published his findings in *Marketing for Nonprofit Organizations* (1975). The seventh edition—*Strategic Marketing for Nonprofit Organizations*—was written with Alan R. Andreasen, and is being used in university marketing classes throughout the country.

Kotler's work gave scientific underpinnings to what successful development officers knew innately and had proven through trial and experiences: There must be a satisfactory exchange at some level between the donor and the nonprofit for both individual and organizational needs to be met. The needs being met will be different than those in the for-profit world. When one is buying a car, for example, and finds the one that makes the heart beat faster just imagining oneself behind the wheel, a number of needs are about to be met between the individual buying the car and dealership, salesman, and, at some point, mechanics. If the car performs well, then there have been multiple satisfactory exchanges.

For an exchange to be satisfactory with a nonprofit, other mental and emotional needs are in play. Some find just the right charity to enable them to help others as they or someone close to them (family member, friend) was helped. Some others are compelled because of the suffering they witness that they want to help alleviate. Even others will support a nonprofit because it saves tax dollars, or they want to be part of a group they admire. Suffice to say, the reasons are many and varied, but the particular connectors between each nonprofit and its supporters and prospects must be actively determined and updated.

Therefore, the nonprofit cannot make assumptions about how it is being viewed and its importance. The leadership must purposefully attempt to identify those particular ways that it meets the needs of its clients, societies, and constituents. Only then can the proper messages be written and tested with the organization's constituencies both to confirm and refine them. More about the methods will be covered later.

DEVELOPMENT IS HOLISTIC

Successful development does not begin and end in the development office. Just as everything you do as an organization to fulfill your mission is integral to the development process, so is every staff member, every board member, and every volunteer. The importance of creating and maintaining an organizational environment that facilitates raising friends and funds cannot be overstated.

The responsibility for building and keeping a productive environment rests with the CEO and the management team. It is "trickle-down" marketing, because what is important to the boss becomes a priority for everyone. There must be an organization-wide understanding and commitment to making certain that everyone—client, student, patient, parent, friend, and so on—who comes in contact with the staff and facility has a positive experience.

In the for-profit world, one outstanding example of creating a positive environment for employees and the public is the Fortune 500 company Owens & Minor. Hugh Gouldthorpe, senior vice president of Quality & Communications, refers to himself as the "head cheerleader" and he has nurtured a welcoming and friendly corporate spirit. Their receptionists have titles that identify them as "directors of first impressions." They answer the phone with the cheerful greeting: "Thank you for calling Owens & Minor. This is *name*. How can I make you smile today?" Should the nonprofit world do less?

When I became the chief development officer at a small liberal arts college in the mid-1970s, the institution had just begun an $8 million capital campaign. To that time, the college had not raised $1 million in any previous effort, and there was skepticism within the board of trustees as to whether the goal was realistically achievable. Of course, the board had voted to approve the campaign but only because the president wanted to do it.

One uneventful day, a check for $100 arrived from an individual who was not in our database. We looked thoroughly, including the president's office files, and it was there that we found a thank-you letter to the donor from a previous president. Curious, we called to thank the donor and to learn more about him and the reason for the gift. He was a graduate of a small Virginia seminary that had become part of the college many years before, and he considered himself an alumnus. He agreed to a meeting with the president on one of his trips to the individual's city, and a firm date was arranged. More productive meetings followed until he agreed to make a $1 million commitment to the college. This estate-related pledge eventually provided more than $4.5 million to the college's endowment following the deaths of the donor and his wife.

The million-dollar commitment was a game-changer for the college and the campaign. It immediately changed perceptions about what was appropriate to give to the college, and spurred us to complete the campaign on time with a bit more than $8 million. This story's happy ending, though, had its beginnings before the $100 check was mailed.

Unknown to us at the time, the donor and his wife visited the campus. The grass was cut, the shrubbery trimmed, the floors were polished. When the couple asked a student if he could point the way to a building, the student, instead, walked them to the destination. Lunch in the snack shop gave them the chance to talk with a few faculty members who were positive about their employment and the college. It was after this pleasant, affirming experience on campus that the donor baited his hook with $100 and cast it to see how we would respond.

Who raised the money? The answer, of course, is that there were many people and factors in enabling a successful solicitation of the college's first million dollar donor in addition to the president and development staff—students, faculty, and the buildings and grounds staff members. Failure in any of these, and the opportunity might not have been presented to us.

There are other examples that could be related from hospitals to churches that provide lessons, both positive and negative. But, the leadership of every nonprofit has a responsibility to make certain the good work being done by one department is being supported by the actions of other departments. Students can become problem alumni because of encounters with the business office or book store. Patients and their families have refused to support hospitals due to treatment at admitting or emergency rooms or by custodial staff members regardless of the care they received from doctors and nurses.

DEVELOPMENT *INCLUDES* FUNDRAISING

Some years ago, the hospital president, the chief development officer, and I were having a discussion about the funding needs that must be achieved during the coming fiscal year, and the capital needs that would have to be met in the next few years. Preparation to make the case for giving to the hospital foundation was nearing completion, so it was important that the supportive material include those items that the hospital truly must have to keep current with medical science and to provide state-of-the-art services to patients.

Frustration was clearly growing in the president's voice and face as she was pressed for concrete answers. She was, unfortunately, having great difficulty identifying areas for funding that year that would not be included in next year's budget. The "needs" were a moving target. Finally, in desperation, she said: "Well, there's money out there! Go raise it!"

This is an extreme example of a common problem for development officers—the expectation that at least some of the objectives of the fundraising program be created in the development office rather than by the organization's leadership. The directive to "go forth and raise money" seems logical to those who do not understand how a successful development program is built. Except for a current, meaningful, and memorable mission statement, there is no more important activity than the process used in setting the near-term and longer-term funding objectives. These objectives, ideally, should come from a serious strategic planning activity where the organization's leadership, along with key volunteers and prospective donors, learn, discuss, and determine the priorities that must be addressed for the organization to work toward fulfilling its mission of service. When these priorities are approved by the governing board, then the development professionals can confidently present the case for support to the organization's constituency with integrity and confidence. In addition, donors can be assured that their financial support will be meaningful in helping to move the organization forward in addressing the needs of those it serves.

Development, properly understood and implemented, addresses the ability of the whole organization—from mission through staffing—to be successful. In practical terms, development professionals responsible for meeting the goals that the organization's leadership has established create annual action plans that incorporate:

- **Marketing/communications**—telling the organization's story to build an accurate perception of its mission, purpose, program, and effectiveness in service and help the target markets understand how their needs are met through their engagement with the organization
- **Fundraising**—meeting the identified financial needs of the organization through effective use of volunteers, activities, and programs to raise voluntary gift support for annual and capital purposes

THE DEVELOPMENT TEAM

Inherent in human nature is the desire to have someone else do those tasks that are outside of our comfort zone—that place in which we feel most competent, at ease, and able to function without concern or fear. It is not surprising, therefore, that the CEOs of a number of nonprofit organizations are eager to hire a "professional fundraiser" to whom can be assigned the responsibility for making the important "ask" for major gifts. Most important to these CEOs is that they be minimally involved in the process.

This attitude, while far too prevalent, is based on a misunderstanding of how and why individuals decide to give money. It is also evidence of a fundamental problem—that of emphasizing the *act of raising money* (sales) rather than the *total development* (marketing) of the organization.

Since development functions primarily through telling your organization's story to build an accurate perception and endorsement of its mission, purpose, program, and effectiveness—it is through this ongoing process that individuals can assess the importance to themselves and their families of your organization and its work, and by that, decide whether or not to participate in its support.

At the center of the marketing/communications and fundraising effort is the nonprofit's president or executive director. He or she personifies your organization in the minds of the public, and is the one who must visibly carry the messages concerning effectiveness and needs to key constituents, provide direction and motivation to board members, and be involved in most calls for major gifts. The CEO cannot effectively hand this responsibility off to anyone else.

It is fair now to ask what should be expected of development officers. Does everyone else do their job while they play golf? The answer, of course, is that successful development officers are effective managers and motivators of other staff members and volunteers. They understand that organizational goals can only be met by a team effort that relies on the involvement and support of the CEO coupled with that of the board—the organization's chief volunteers. They create, with the participation and agreement of the board, the annual development action plan to raise the friends and funds the organization requires and work with the CEO, staff, and volunteers in implementing it. They make calls and ask for money, but they understand that they can be more productive working through others. This especially applies in helping the CEO become the successful major fundraiser that is demanded by the nature of the position.

Good development officers offer individuals the opportunity to invest in human energy and talent and to help guide succeeding generations toward positive futures. Such development officers divert the spotlight away from themselves and cause it to shine on volunteers, the CEO, and board members. Successful development officers help others achieve their goals, and, in so doing, meet the marketing/communications and financial goals of the organizations they serve.

THE COMPONENTS OF SUCCESSFUL DEVELOPMENT PROGRAMS

In the chapters that follow, we will discuss in detail the basic components of building and operating a successful development program. Raising friends and funds can only be successful when your nonprofit has:

- A clear understanding of what it is and who it serves
- A strategic vision and clearly defined objectives
- The ownership of the vision and objectives by its board members and other key volunteers
- An internal statement of the case for support
- A written plan for marketing and communications
- A means for utilizing volunteers in meaningful ways
- A well-designed program to raise annual funds and major gifts both during lifetime and through estate-related giving
- A recordkeeping system that enables the development program to function more easily
- An aware, committed, and involved governing board
- A CEO who understands and is committed to fulfilling his or her role in the total development program
- A well-trained and motivated development staff

We will also attempt to reinforce the broader, comprehensive understanding and approach to development—that everyone associated with your organization and everything your nonprofit does has a positive or negative impact on your ability to be successful. It is when this reality becomes part of your organizational culture that your mission will truly come to life in your community of service.

CHAPTER 2

A Clear and Compelling Mission

"If you didn't exist, would somebody invent you?" That question was appropriately asked many times during the remarkable career of the late Dr. Robert Stuhr, a good friend and mentor. The question was and is not meant to be impudent, but to cause organizational leadership to think seriously about the reason the nonprofit exists and functions today. Do the needs the organization was created to meet still require the same attention? What has changed? Have the clients and program changed without revising the mission statement? Do board members know what the mission is?

A corollary to the above question is: "What do board and staff members *believe* your mission to be?" Sometimes the problem is that the very length of the mission statement makes it difficult to remember. At other times, the mission was not properly introduced to each new board and staff member, assuming that they already knew or would find out by reading the materials they were given.

A good exercise to discover what your board and staff members know about your mission is this: At an appropriate meeting of each group, pass out a half sheet of paper, asking each person to write down what he or she believes is the mission of the organization. The results will provide fodder for productive discussions, and may set the stage for a review of the mission statement.

At a nonprofit some years ago, just such an experiment was conducted with board and staff members, to determine if they could articulate the sense of the mission, if not the exact wording. The nonprofit was engaged in a variety of services to the inner city, from alternative education to pregnancy counseling. The list grew over time because the executive director encouraged staff members to try new ideas, no matter whether they necessarily flowed from the mission statement. It became important, however, to be able to communicate correctly the organization to its own constituents and to engage others in knowledge and support of the nonprofit to know how the chief volunteers (the board) were talking about the organization to friends, colleagues, fellow country club members, Rotarians, etc. Therefore, at a board meeting, members were given a slip of paper and asked to write down the mission statement. These responses were collected and revealed that not one board member was correct, and no two answers were the same. Knowing this, the nonprofit began to be serious about defining itself in terms of the reality of what it had become.

When beginning to provide consulting services or conducting development audits for clients, it is always important to interview each board member individually. The first question asked concerns the members' understanding of the nonprofit's mission. The answers to that question provide an especially revealing insight into the organization's ability to define, fund, and operate its programs of service.

Lack of understanding and miscommunication of the mission statement is the more common problem. Sometimes, though, there is precise understanding of the mission on the part of the leadership but a steadfast unwillingness to change the nonprofit's mission in spite of new realities. The unwillingness to change, adapt, and expand thinking about dealing with new possibilities have resulted in organizational demise.

Mission statements are normally reviewed, edited, or changed as part of strategic planning that occurs every three to five years. However, the environment in which nonprofits operate is changing more quickly today than in previous times. It is critical that every nonprofit review its mission statement annually to make certain that it accurately and briefly describes who you are and why you are.

An effective mission statement should always be as succinct and poignant as possible, and no more than fifteen words. Longer than that, and board and staff members and other volunteers will not be able to remember it. One of the best presently being used is that of Second Baptist Church in Richmond, VA: "A loving community, transformed by Christ, for unbounded service." Some of the worst are contained in college catalogues, many of which go on for several pages. As an exercise, pick up almost any college catalogue, read the mission and highlight the key words that get at the main reason the institution exists. Applicants and parents should not have to work that hard, however, to learn why that higher educational institution is special.

The mission statement is just that—a simple statement about the core reason your organization was created, written in plain language that is easy to be understood and remembered. Anything other than that (explanations, bullet points, etc.) is just clutter that obscures the reality of why you are and who you serve.

CREATING/RE-CREATING YOUR MISSION STATEMENT

There is more than one approach to analyzing and either confirming your mission or writing a new one. Usually, there is a sense on the part of the CEO and other top staff members that the mission statement is unwieldy, unmemorable, or not descriptive of the organization's current program and emphasis. In rare instances, one or more board members will raise the issue. In any case, when this realization occurs, these methods can be productive:

- An ad hoc committee can be appointed by the chair of the board to review and create a new mission statement to be recommended to the board at a certain future date. The committee can be configured in a number of ways, but likely will include the CEO, the chief development officer, and a couple of board members. The chair of the board is always an ex-official member of all board committees. Sometimes, others are added to the mix from students or clients served as well as one or two key supporters.

- The full board and top staff members, usually in an annual retreat, can be used either to review/confirm the mission or to rewrite it.

- The strategic planning committee is the most usual group to examine the mission statement as one of the first orders of business. Since the mission is the basis for everything in which a nonprofit is engaged, it is vital to make certain this foundational statement is in place before moving to setting strategic objectives.

Whichever method is chosen for your organization, it is helpful to have one person serve as a facilitator or bring an experienced facilitator in from the outside. A good technique to begin is to ask each person in the group—individually and one at a time—to give one word that describes the mission of the organization. Go around the room in this fashion until all of the words have been exhausted and are written on a board or flip chart for all to see. You will notice similarities between some of the descriptive words, and the facilitator will help bring consensus around the fundamental words that should make up the mission statement.

A number of organizations have a mission statement and a "vision" statement. In the view of this writer, one good mission statement is all any organization needs. Usually, the impetus for creating a vision statement comes from the feeling that something is missing from the mission.

USING THE MISSION STATEMENT

When you have created the right mission statement, you want everyone to know it—and it can be used in a number of ways. Some of these are:

- In or near the masthead of your hard copy and e-mail publications
- Posted within your organization at key spots where staff, clients, and visitors will see it

- Speaking it at the beginning of board and other volunteer committee meetings
- Addressing it when making presentations to civic and religious groups, explaining how it is being given life through the organization's work
- Discussing every program of the nonprofit in terms of how it is helping to meet the organization's mission

THE GOOD, THE BAD, AND THE UGLY

Previously, you were given an example of an excellent mission statement in use by Second Baptist Church of Richmond, VA. The following are our opinions of mission statements that are effective and those that need work.

1. The first example comes from a nonprofit located outside the United States.

   Mission Statement

   X is committed to create a broad-based, interactive, and unified community dedicated to assist underserved and less fortunate children of low-income and indigent families to help themselves complete their education and achieve economic self-sufficiency through access to educational assistance, child development services, health care and support services to become positive, self-esteemed individuals with high moral values on which to build a successful life.

   Vision Statement

   X will be the leading organization that bridges the gap between the deserving children and the resources that allow them to attain the education they fully deserve.

   This worthwhile organization has crafted a mission statement that only the executive director could love—and remember. On the other hand, the Vision Statement encapsulates much more precisely why the organization exists and who it lives to serve. When organizations feel the need for a "Vision Statement," it is usually an indictment of the mission statement.

2. A cultural arts center provides the second example.

   Mission Statement

   The mission of the Y Cultural Arts Center is to encourage and advocate the visual and performing arts by providing a forum where diverse audiences can actively participate in cultural experiences.

   The Y Cultural Arts Center is committed to supporting the economic vitality of (city) by enhancing the life experiences of our citizens and visitors.

In this case, the Center is on the right track, but still the leadership should revisit the mission statement to bring the two sentences together and provide both clarity and focus. A possible revision is:

The Y Cultural Arts Center is committed to encouraging and advocating the visual and performing arts to enhance the life experience of our citizens and visitors.

Granted, the financial benefits of the Center are not in the rewritten statement, but it could be argued that by working toward fulfilling its primary mission, economic benefits will necessarily follow.

3. An organization that promotes music and culture gives us example number three.

    Mission Statement

    Our mission is to promote, preserve, perpetuate, and encourage the music, arts, culture and heritage of communities in (state) through festivals, programs and other cultural, educational, civic, and economic activities.

    This statement is a bit wordy, but it does attempt to address the heart and soul of the organization. It could be simplified as follows and still get the point across.

    Our mission is to promote, preserve, perpetuate, and encourage the music, arts, culture and heritage of communities throughout (state).

    How it will accomplish the mission should be left out of the statement because the means will always be a variable.

4. The fourth example is from a very young recreation organization.

    Mission Statement

    ABC's mission is to provide recreational experiences on three different levels (recreation, challenge, and tournament), that will help our young people learn the fundamentals of baseball and softball, and exhibit good sportsmanship at all times while growing into healthier and happier adults.

    This statement is fairly direct, but still tries to say too much. Again, the "how" is included with the "why," and that both complicates the statement and restricts the possibilities for the organization. Here is a suggested revision.

    ABC will provide recreational experiences that will help young people learn fundamental skills and good sportsmanship while growing into healthier and happier adults.

5. The last illustration is from an agency that serves inner city youth.

    Mission Statement

    Our mission is to support the intellectual, physical, spiritual, and emotional development of children so they become self-sufficient, contributing members of the community.

The statement is slightly more than the fifteen-word ideal, but it has the clarity and focus that all good mission statements should possess. This organization also has a vision statement that is, basically, a restatement of the mission and completely unnecessary.

IN SUMMARY

Before you find and read your organization's mission statement, try reciting it from memory. Then, write down what you think it is (no fair peeking). Finally, you can read the mission and compare it to what you thought and wrote. Being off in a word or two does not count—you have the essence of your mission in mind. However, if you have had too much difficulty remembering or are completely off-target, you have identified a problem, but one that also presents you and your organization with an opportunity.

At your next board meeting, put a discussion of the mission statement on the agenda. Ask each board member to write down in his or her own words the mission of the organization they collectively own. Once they have finished, reveal on a flip chart or other display the current mission statement. The ensuing discussion may be one of the most productive your board will have had for some time. There can be no more important task for your or any organization than making certain the mission is clear, coherent, compelling, and brief.

Each chapter that follows will discuss and provide guidance on the construction and operation of a successful program to engage your publics and solicit their support. However, none of these will work for your organization without an accurate, compelling, and memorable statement of your mission. When that is right, and your programs flow from it, your development program will be built on the foundation of coherence and truth.

CHAPTER 3

Building Ownership through Planning

There would be a general agreement that every nonprofit organization needs a strategic plan that lays out the vision, goals, and objectives to be achieved in a specified time period. Most, in fact, could produce their current strategic plans upon request, with different reports on the success of their implementation. Some have set up a method of monitoring the progress being made and send regular reports to staff and board members. Others will blow the accumulation of dust from their plans and admit that very little was done following the perfunctory approval by the board.

The process used to create the strategic plan is the best predictor of whether or not the goals and objectives will be seriously pursued and accomplished. If the creation of the plan is viewed as a pivotal opportunity to obtain understanding, acceptance, and ownership of your organizational goals and objectives among a broad cross-section of staff and board members, major prospects, and other key persons within your constituency, the prognosis for success in implementation are markedly better.

On the other hand, if the plan is written by an internal group of staff members with the input primarily from the CEO and, perhaps, a few members of the board, the outcome is most likely to be disappointing. Building ownership at this most basic stage of development is a significant step toward achieving the funding goals necessary for your organization's success. Properly conceived and implemented, the strategic planning process can:

- Bring a fresh perspective to the proposed projects being considered.
- Uncover and deal with perceptions that may hinder your ability to raise major dollars.
- Cultivate board members and other major prospects who will be needed to contribute major gifts.

- Develop committed volunteer leadership for fundraising.
- Develop new candidates for board membership.

ELEMENTS OF SUCCESSFUL PLANNING

A strategic plan is a written expression of the shared vision of the leadership and representatives of the community that comprises your organization. The strategic plan is your blueprint, stating in a logical way where your organization has been, where it is now, where it should be going, and what resources will be required to get it there. The successful planning process involves four steps:

1. Where is the organization at the present time?
   - Gather all the facts—financial and program.
   - Conduct a SWOT analysis.
   - Identify priorities.
2. What should be your organizational direction?
   - Explore various ways of dealing with issues identified through the SWOT exercise.
   - Determine the current mission and objectives to meet it.
3. How does your organization accomplish these objectives?
   - Discuss and devise strategies (strengthen development program, capital campaign).
   - Determine resources needed for each strategic move, including operating budget.
4. How does your organization keep on target and evaluate its progress?
   - Write an action plan based on the objectives.
   - Set up a system of frequent reporting, measuring progress against time line.
   - Adjust action plan and/or objectives as new information is received.

The diagram in Figure 3.1 shows the flow and the continuity of the strategic planning process.

As can be seen by the diagram, strategic planning is not confined to the planning activity itself. It is truly a process that moves through stages until the next planning activity begins.

ESTABLISHING THE STRATEGIC PLANNING COMMITTEE

The strategic planning process is significant for your organization and should be entered into in a serious way. The first step is to set up an ad hoc committee

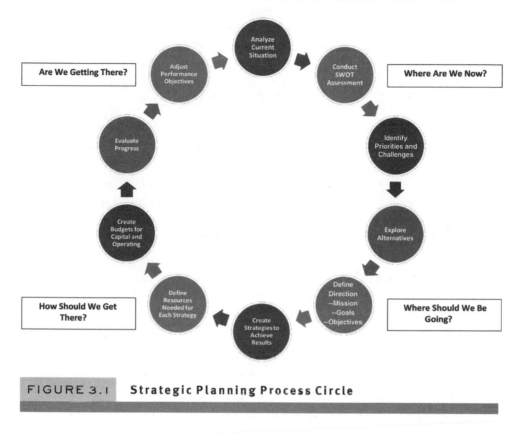

Are We Getting There?

Where Are We Now?

How Should We Get There?

Where Should We Be Going?

FIGURE 3.1   Strategic Planning Process Circle

comprising the CEO, board chair, chief development officer, and the board vice chair of development. This small group should determine the constituencies to be represented on the strategic planning committee and select the prospective members to be recruited. In order to do this, the committee will establish those categories under which prospective committee members can be listed—staff and faculty members, physicians, political, business, professional, members of your important constituent groups, major prospects/donors, and so forth. It is very important that those selected for the strategic planning committee be individuals who have the knowledge, influence, and resources to achieve the vision that the plan will express.

Next, the ad hoc committee should draft and approve the job description for the strategic planning committee, and establish the action steps and time line—from recruitment of members to the finalization of the plan. At this point, it is often helpful to submit the prospective committee names, job description, and the action time line to the board for review and approval. The more the entire leadership moves together even in creating the process, the more likely will the end product be accepted.

The ad hoc committee members will then have the task of inviting prospective members to participate in the planning process. A good technique is to send a letter of invitation with the promise of a follow-up phone call to answer questions and get their agreement. The model suggested here would require a commitment to attend and participate in three meetings of a specified time over a six-week period. Those familiar with other strategic planning models may be surprised by this compressed time, but it has been successfully used by a number of disparate organizations. The advantage, of course, is that individuals know that they are making a limited commitment with a time certain when it will conclude. In addition, the compressed time period for planning forces concentration on the planning activity.

In most cases, the strategic planning committee meetings can be kept to two-hour blocks of time, though this will vary depending upon the nature and complexity of the organization.

CONDUCTING THE STRATEGIC PLANNING COMMITTEE MEETINGS

For the strategic planning process to be productive, three principles should kept before the committee:

1. The vision of your organization must be clearly articulated by the CEO.
2. The committee should be encouraged to concentrate on what your organization needs to achieve in order to fulfill its mission and reach toward its potential.
3. The questions "What are we becoming?" and "What should we become?" should be central to the planning activity.

Each of the three meetings of the strategic planning committee has a particular and distinctive purpose, and the facilitator must make certain that the members adhere to the purpose of the meeting.

Meeting One is designed to set the stage for the planning to come. Information is shared by the CEO, financial officer, and others to make certain that the members have complete data on the current status of the organization. Any question asked or requested information not available at the meeting must be provided to the committee members before the next session. Since the CEO is the visible embodiment of the organization, she or he should be clear about the challenges and the vision held for the nonprofit in the future. It is during this meeting that the mission statement is reviewed/edited/changed, and a SWOT (Strengths, Weaknesses, Opportunities, Threats) analysis is conducted, giving members the opportunity to define the environment for setting the objectives to help the nonprofit meet its mission.

Meeting Two enables members of the committee to summarize data and begin setting priorities. The committee is divided into small groups for this purpose, and a report is made from each small group, regarding their list of objectives and the reasons for the selections. Before the meeting ends, each member is given the charge of individually selecting their 1st, 2nd, and 3rd priorities. No decisions are made through this preliminary activity.

During Meeting Three, the strategic planning committee finalizes its recommendations that will be sent to the governing board for review and approval. The committee will also provide suggestions as to the means to achieve objectives that will require raising additional funds. Sometimes, a capital campaign will be recommended; at other times, a more energetic fundraising program will be required.

MANAGING THE PLAN AND ACHIEVING YOUR OBJECTIVES

Once the strategic plan has been created, written, and approved by the board, the real work begins. This is not the time to celebrate, put the plan on the shelf, and move on to other tasks. A plan gathering dust does nothing to advance your organization toward meeting its mission. It must become the energy behind your actions and expressed through the priorities you establish in your annual operating budget and planning.

Members of your board should play important roles in paying attention to achieving the strategic objectives. It is good practice for the chair of the board to set up a committee of board and staff members to develop an action plan that adheres to the time frames in the strategic plan, assign tasks, and take steps to accelerate the plan and/or make necessary adjustments. While not possible at every organization, appointing a board member and an appropriate staff member responsible for each objective emphasizes the importance of the work and clearly establishes accountability. Whether or not such assignments are made, reports on progress should be on the agenda of every board meeting and written reports should be circulated to relevant staff members.

PLANNING FOR A CAPITAL CAMPAIGN

Given that many organizations use an internal planning process involving board and staff members (at times, only staff members), and the result of the deliberations point toward a capital campaign, the planning process described above can be successfully adapted to plan and build ownership of capital goals.

A number of years ago, a private girls' school in the Midwest with which we began working had developed a strategic plan using the usual suspects—

administrative staff, some faculty, and a few members of the board. The conclusion of this effort was an accumulation of objectives that, if achieved, would require raising several million dollars. The problem, of course, was that the only ones who owned the objectives were the members of the internal planning committee, the enthusiastic faculty, and school administration. Not even board members who had financial resources were convinced that the plan made sense.

In normal circumstances, the school would have paid for a feasibility study to determine the level of interest of the proposed campaign goals and the institution's internal ability to run a capital effort. However, the leadership already knew that its major prospects did not have the necessary level of "buy in" even though they had the money to give. We suggested that, since the obstacle was building understanding and appreciation of the funding objectives, the school invite key individuals to participate in a campaign-planning activity based on the recommendations of the strategic plan. The Headmaster and chief development officer agreed. The resulting Campaign Planning Committee was comprised of board members and non-board members in equal numbers, selected with care by the director of development.

When the meetings began, several members of the board wondered why the school was going through this process. One remarked, after hearing that a campaign goal might total more than $2 million, that no one will give that much to a girls' school. Another thought it was a complete waste of time, but he agreed to participate because he was a member of the board. The result:

- The campaign total agreed upon was $15 million.
- The committee member who did not think anyone would give generously to a girl's school made the motion to approve the goal.
- The board member who thought his time was being wasted made a challenge commitment of $1 million if other board members would give $2 million.
- The campaign co-chairs came from non-board members serving on the campaign planning committee—one of whom eventually became chair of the board.
- The board approved and launched a successful capital campaign.

This method of planning capital campaigns has been used with success at a number of nonprofits over the last 15 years. The technique is not meant to be a replacement for feasibility studies in all cases—sometimes a combination of a study and planning are necessary—but only to emphasize that in every case, building ownership among those who are needed for your funding goals to be met is of vital importance.

IN SUMMARY

How the planning process is constructed and conducted will facilitate or make more difficult accomplishing strategic objectives. Using a broad-based approach that includes individuals of influence whose involvement in creating the plan will improve the ability of your organization to achieve its funding goals. There are risks of involving those beyond the board and faculty/staff because the initial vision of your leadership will be changed—and usually improved. Building ownership among those who can give and influence others to give should be powerful motivation to engage their opinions and input in a meaningful way. Once they convince themselves, many will become major donors and leadership volunteers.

THE STRATEGIC PLANNING PROCESS

Target Dates   **Chronological Steps**

_____   1. Proposal from the executive director to the development committee of the board on the appointment of a strategic planning committee.

_____   2. Recommendation from the development committee to the board that a strategic planning committee be appointed including job description and timetable for committee's work.

_____   3. Selection and recruitment of membership of the strategic planning committee. Membership should include persons with means to enable campaign's success.

_____   4. The strategic planning committee performs its task of:
   a. Reviewing the mission and purpose of the organization
   b. Analyzing the strengths, weaknesses, opportunities, and threats
   c. Reaching consensus on the objectives to be accomplished within three years to fulfill its mission
   d. Recommending the overall strategy to achieve the objectives

_____   5. Recommendation of the strategic planning committee is submitted to the board for approval.

_____   6. Acceptance of the report by the board.

_____   7. Discussion and approval of all or part of the recommendations contained in the report:
   a. Program and staffing recommendations that can be achieved within the current budget

b. Recommendations that require additional resources through the development program

_____ 8. Drafting of the case statement. The process should involve key members of the institution's community as well as members of the board.

_____ 9. Preliminary approval of the case statement by the board.

_____ 10. Building ownership through individual and small group meetings of the strategic plan and the development initiatives.

_____ 11. Final approval of the strategic plan, the development plan, and the case statement.

STRATEGIC PLANNING COMMITTEE JOB DESCRIPTION

The formation of the strategic planning committee was authorized by the board of trustees. The committee has been charged with the responsibility of thoroughly examining the mission and purpose of (Name of Organization) and recommending the direction of the organization for the next three to five years. It is expected that the recommendations would be in the form of objectives to be accomplished within a specified period of time.

The membership of the strategic planning committee will include representation from the broad spectrum of (Name of Organization)'s constituency. Groups represented will be: Members of the board of directors, and key staff (church, medicine, education, community, business leaders, etc.).

The committee will:

1. Review, study and become thoroughly knowledgeable with reports and other documents, which will assist it in analyzing the current status of (Name of Organization) and how it came to this point.

2. Consider if the mission and purpose are still current and compelling—confirm if they are and change them if they are not.

3. Based on the mission, consider the needs of the organization for program, capital improvements, and endowment.

4. Prioritize these needs and place them in a framework of time.

5. Make its report containing recommendations and rationale to the board of directors by (Date) _____.

It is intended that the strategic planning committee accomplish its task during three meetings to be held at (location) on the following dates and times: _____

It is tentatively planned that the meetings of the committee would be organized as follows:

The first meeting will be an opportunity to consider the mission statement and to conduct a SWOT analysis. Also, reports and other material would be presented to provide members with as complete a picture as possible of the organization as it exists today and how it came to this point.

The second meeting will enable committee members to begin the process of identifying needs and prioritizing them.

At the third meeting, it is intended that decisions would be made regarding priorities. The mission statement would be completed. The report would be ready for drafting. A fourth meeting would be scheduled only if absolutely necessary. The remaining work of reviewing and approving the written report would be done by mail and teleconference.

STRATEGIC PLANNING COMMITTEE MEETING AGENDAS

I.   The strategic planning process
   A. The Vision for the organization must be clearly put forth by the executive director.
   B. The committee should concentrate on what the organization needs to achieve in order to fulfill its mission and reach toward its potential.
   C. The questions "What are we becoming?" and "What should we become?" should be central to the planning process.

II.   Meeting One
   A. The principal purpose of this meeting is informational—bringing the committee up-to-date on the history/traditions, current program, vision, etc.
   B. Agenda may be as follows:
      1. Welcome and purpose of the meeting
      2. Presentation on the history and future of the organization
         a. Executive director's opportunity to talk about her vision. Uses other staff members to give information about finances, development, program, etc.
         b. Important for the executive director to be a controlling coordinator of this portion of the meeting.
         c. Facts and figures are distributed to support presentations.
      3. Conduct a SWOT analysis
      4. Discussion and questions

V. Meeting Two
    A. The principal task is to discuss what was learned during Meeting One and begin the process of planning the organization's future. A number of possibilities within different time frames will be considered, but nothing is finalized.
    B. The agenda may be as follows:
       1. Welcome and purposes of the meeting
       2. Discussion/questions/answers from Meeting One
       3. Small group brainstorming to list objectives for the next three years
          a. Needs that may have been presented and suggested at previous meeting have been categorized in three lists—facilities, program, endowment
          b. Useful to have a flip chart for each small group to record suggestions, priorities, etc.
       4. Initial prioritizations by the planning committee members

VI. Meeting Three
    A. The committee will review the priorities identified in the previous meeting, reach a consensus on the key strategic objectives, and recommend the method(s) of achieving these objectives. The recommendations will be presented to the board for its approval.
    B. The agenda may be as follows:
       1. Welcome and purpose of the meeting
       2. Presentation of the alternative ideas discussed at the previous meeting
       3. Final prioritization of needs and adoption of goals
       4. Consideration of methods of meeting goals
       5. Adoption of report and recommendations to the board

CHAPTER 4

Creating the Case for Support

A number of years ago, a college president conducted a campus tour for a visiting friend. While showing the friend the buildings and grounds, the president could not resist talking about his plans for capital improvement in the next several years. Here, he proclaimed, will be a new performing arts center; there, will rise a state-of-the-art science building. He went on at some length about the plans he had to meet the college's needs and expand its possibilities.

His friend listened patiently, admiringly, and mostly quietly, except for an occasional "Oh," and "Won't that be great." Finally, when they had returned to where they had begun the excursion, the friend asked a simple but profound question: "Who else shares your vision for the college?" There was silence for a noticeable time. Then, the president said, "I don't know. But I'm sure that everyone will agree with me."

The well-meaning president committed the common sin of "assumption." His vision of the college was so completely developed in his mind as the best possible course for his institution that he could not imagine anyone not agreeing with him—let alone having ideas of their own. So, it fell to his good friend to guide him back to reality. Unless the president becomes independently wealthy, he must reveal his vision to those who can help him bring it to fruition. He must engage them in dialogue about the college's future and, in the subsequent give-and-take, together he and they will develop a shared vision whose broad ownership will help ensure its fulfillment.

As we discussed in the previous chapter, creating a vision and building ownership begins with a process that invites key representatives of your constituents to work with board members, administration, and staff members in defining organizational priorities. Following that strategic planning process, an internal statement of the case for support should be created.

THE INTERNAL CASE STATEMENT—BASIC DEVELOPMENT TOOL

An internal case statement has many purposes, but chief among them is to make certain that your organization crafts and expresses its message in a way that elicits agreement among all principal persons in your organization. When you get everyone on the same page, staff and volunteers will have a coherent and unifying story that will be directed to the communities who are important to you. The result will probably be a bit different than the original ideas the president dreamed, but the results will have the distinct advantage of having the support of those who are needed to achieve the goals.

The internal case statement, like the late comedian Rodney Dangerfield, often does not get the full measure of respect it deserves. It can be long, is filled with data, and is not pretty. Yet, it serves as the very foundation of your marketing and fundraising effort, whether it undergirds a capital campaign or the on-going effort to raise funds and friends.

Given that the internal case statement, among other things, is a marketing document, the process of creation also enables you to clarify more specifically the answers to the question: *"If you didn't exist, would somebody invent you?"* This question is not only important in crafting the essence of your nonprofit in the mission statement, but must be asked again as you bore down to the compelling reasons that your organization exists today—not last year or even when it was founded. Developing a clear statement of why you are relevant today helps your constituencies understand why their needs are being met by supporting your organization with their time and money.

Once the internal case statement is completed, CEO, development personnel, and volunteers can use it as a resource in the preparation of foundation proposals, fundraising brochures, general presentational materials for speeches, presentations to inform new prospects, and other developmentally useful publications.

Remember, it is vital that this process involve developing a consensus internally among the rest of the board, the other administrators, and remainder of the staff (including faculty, medical staff, etc.)—all persons central to telling the story and raising funds for your organization. This is accomplished through the process of preparing the internal statement case for support.

The ***Internal Case Statement*** is used in the following ways:

1. To achieve an internal consensus among board, staff, and principal volunteers of the manner and the language used to describe the organization and the development program.

    Your organization measurably increases its chances for success in fundraising when the projects and programs to be funded are understood, owned, and supported by your internal constituency. As we have already said, leadership may believe that everyone will agree with the charted directions, but are often surprised to learn that not enough time has been spent discussing and seeking input on the development goals with those who actually provide the services. Some members of the staff may have differing ideas—maybe even good ones—and will resent not being asked for their reactions and suggestions. Others who agree with everything you want to do may still feel disenfranchised or unappreciated. In every case, morale is decidedly not improved.

2. To serve as the basic resource document for the fundraising program.

   The internal case statement is not meant for general consumption, though various parts of it will appear in a number of fundraising pieces—from individual proposals to campaign brochures. Preparing the internal case statement provides the opportunity to collect all the pertinent data on your organization—from financial information to the square footage of current facilities—and finally have it in one place. Once you get the information, make certain that you update it on a regular basis.

3. To create external materials for marketing, public relations, and fundraising.

   Besides raw data, the internal case statement contains the story of your organization, its current position, what it needs/wants to do, and the financial challenges that must be met to fulfill its mission. Since the document has gone through an internal vetting process, you can be confident in using the language of the case statement in preparing the materials that will be used in describing your organization and its needs to your constituents and the general public.

4. To play an important role in testing the market.

   The executive summary of the case statement and, at times, a presentational version in PowerPoint, can be greatly useful in testing with selected constituents how well and clearly your organizational story has been told, what is still missing for the case statement to be compelling, and assessing their supportive interest. When used in combination with a prospect identification program, it is possible to build a list of potential suspects and prospects for your organization. No matter what you may initially create and how proud you feel about your accomplishment, nothing should be considered final until your case statement is tested with individuals beyond your inner circle.

5. To recruit and inspire volunteer leadership.

   Selectively using the internal case statement with key prospective volunteers can help in enlisting their help with your fundraising program. Top volunteer leadership wants to know that the organization they are helping approaches its work in a thorough and well-organized way. When combined with an executive summary, the internal case statement can serve as a compelling support document in giving a volunteer confidence your organization will give him or her support needed to succeed.

6. To assist in raising major "lead" gifts.

Of course, top volunteer leaders are most often prospects for major gifts. Therefore, the recruitment and solicitation process, using the internal case statement, can be very effective with certain of your prospects—though not all. Just the knowledge that the complete document exists, along with an executive summary for the volunteer's consumption, will be enough information for most.

WHAT THE INTERNAL CASE STATEMENT INCLUDES

The internal case statement, as has been said, is an inclusive development resource that will be used in the creation of materials as divergent as annual fund brochures to foundation proposals. It exists as the story of what your nonprofit was, what it is now, what it needs to accomplish, and what is required to succeed.

- Begin at the beginning.
  - Why and how did your organization begin?
  - Who did you serve?
  - Who were the key persons or group of persons that were involved in the founding?
  - What was your anticipated role in society, in education, etc.
  - What were your early significant accomplishments?
  - How and why have you changed?
- What aspects of your organization must be preserved and why?
- If your organization did not exist, would someone invent it?
  - Does your current mission statement describe who you are?
  - How are you fulfilling an important role in your community? In society?
  - How are you distinctive?
  - What are your recent significant accomplishments?
  - How are you sure that your organization is succeeding?
  - How are you measuring your success?
  - What impact are you making on your community, on society, on the church, etc.?

- What have been the physical expansions/contractions of your organization?
  - How has the physical plant developed and in response to what need(s)?
  - How has the (faculty, staff) grown and improved your ability to serve?
  - Is your client/student base growing, stable, or reducing? What are the reasons for this, and what are your projections for the next five years?
  - Have you operated in a fiscally sound manner?
  - Has your constituency provided financial support when needed?
- What do you need to do in the next three to five years in your efforts to fulfill your mission?
  - How did you determine the organization's priorities in programs and facilities?
  - What are the challenges you must face and overcome?
  - What are your current strengths?
  - What opportunities are there?
  - What current weaknesses and threats must be addressed?
- How will you accomplish your objectives?
  - How much money will you have to raise, and for what purposes?
    - Operating/current program support?
    - New construction and/or renovation?
  - Building endowment?
  - When will each objective need to be completed to ensure organizational stability and growth?
  - What will the accomplishment of objectives mean in your ability to fulfill your mission?
- Supporting materials
  - List of the kinds of gifts that will be accepted
  - List of the opportunities to name physical facilities and endowed funds
  - Year-by-year overview of the development program
  - Summary of financial information for previous five years
  - Summary of endowment growth over previous five to ten years
  - Summary of fundraising progress over previous five years
  - Summary of enrollment data for previous five years (colleges and schools)
  - Summary of clients served for previous five years (social service agencies, health care organizations, etc.)
  - Examples of achievement by alumni(ae), faculty, physicians, researchers, professional staff, etc.
  - Lists of the board of trustees, advisory groups, and any other significant volunteer participation

THE PROCESS OF CREATING THE INTERNAL CASE STATEMENT

There are no shortcuts to preparing the internal case statement. However, the benefits of having gone through the process of gathering the data, drafting, and re-drafting this document will be seen throughout your organization. When you are finished, the understanding, acceptance, and appreciation of our organization among board and staff members will have been heightened. Some of you may find that the process will provide education about your organization that it was presumed board members knew, but did not. Furthermore, everyone will be better prepared to carry your nonprofit's message forward to your constituency and the larger community in which you deliver your services.

The first step is to appoint a case statement committee. This can be done by the CEO, by the chair of the board, or jointly. The committee may include the CEO, the chief development officer, the finance officer, the director of marketing/communications, other key staff members (faculty, physician, social worker, etc.), board chair, board development chair, and, if beginning a capital fundraising effort, the chair(s) of the campaign.

At the first meeting of this committee, a member of the staff is assigned to be the principal writer. It does not do any good to try to draft the document by committee, though the members will have ample opportunity to comment on the drafts produced. A list of information necessary to create the first draft is compiled, and committee members are asked to accept appropriate assignments to assemble the data. A time line with intermediate deadlines for completing the document is also reviewed and adopted.

Following this initial meeting, the process normally moves in this fashion:

- The first draft of the internal case system is written and sent to the CEO and chief development officer for review and comments.

- The second draft is prepared and sent to all members of the case statement committee for their comments and editing.

- The third draft is written and sent to key members of the organization's staff (department chairs, cabinet members, etc.) as well as to the case statement committee for additional edits and suggestions.

- The fourth draft is prepared, reviewed by the case statement committee (with minor edits), and approved to be sent to the full board for comments. At this point, it is good practice to send a list of questions along with the draft to help focus the members' review.

- The board approves the internal case statement.

Once approval is obtained, an executive summary can be written, reviewed, and approved by the case statement committee to be used in market testing and cultivation of major prospects.

TIPS FOR THE WRITER

In the world of development, pride of authorship must be repressed in order to do the work and achieve the intended results on behalf of your organization. No matter how elegant you consider your prose to be and how long you may have labored over a word or phrase, it is guaranteed that someone on the reviewing committee will fail to appreciate your literary skills. Remember that your function is to write and shepherd a process that will produce a document that can be used both to tell your organization's story effectively and have the information needed for a variety of marketing and fundraising purposes.

That being said, here a few tips that may help you create just the right master document for your organization:

- Be direct and brief, but also thorough. The most difficult writing is also the simplest and easy to understand. That should be your goal.
- Make certain that all statements are supportable and defensible.
- Your readers want to be inspired, so stress the future of service that your organization can provide by achieving the funding goals.
- Know that the only need that counts is that of the prospective donor. The copy must be written in terms that prospects and donors understand how their needs will be met by meeting the organization's needs.
- Emphasize strengths of your organization and build on them.
- Be positive and optimistic.
- Be both rational and emotional. Let your passion for the mission of your organization shine through the copy.

PREPARING PRESENTATIONAL CASE STATEMENT MATERIALS

The printed materials that will be created from the internal case statement contain more than the words, but add the music as well. It is said that great art is a matter of selectivity and control—knowing what to use and the setting in which it is used. Selecting the internal case statement language depends upon the audience who will be reading it, and the design of the material will assist in delivering your message in a format that is most agreeable to the individuals whose behavior you want to influence. The format may be a booklet, brochure, newsletter, PowerPoint, e-mail, and other mediums. Whichever is chosen must meet the expectations of the target audience and not seem inappropriate to the perception held of the organization. The challenge is creating effective printed materials that will *facilitate* the work of staff members, board members, and other volunteers, both in telling your story and motivating desired behaviors in identified donors and prospects.

The marketing language upon which the leadership of your organization has reached consensus should be used in every venue to tell your organization's story, including online communications and direct mail solicitations. We will discuss marketing in more detail in the following chapter, but we will conclude this one by encouraging you always to stay on message whatever the communication method being used.

In Summary

The internal case statement is the most important marketing and fundraising resource your organization can produce. It is the foundational document that brings all factions of your organization together in language, message, vision, needs, and resources. No one beyond CEO, board, and development staff is meant to see and use the internal case statement except for an executive summary that can be shared with major donors. However, it will serve as an invaluable resource in guaranteeing a consistent message from you nonprofit and giving the development staff confidence in the creation of marketing and fundraising materials.

CHAPTER 5

Telling Your Organization's Story

There is an old saying in development that you can have a marketing program without fundraising, but you cannot have a fundraising program without marketing. This is an acknowledgement of the obvious: You must tell your organization's story to those who should care about your program and services to gain their understanding, acceptance, appreciation—and support—of your work. Your goal is to motivate a growing number of your constituents to become personally involved as a volunteer and to provide voluntary financial support.

Easy for us to say; however, successfully planning and implementing a coherent marketing and communications program often become a difficult proposition. For one thing, staff members and volunteers—let alone your larger constituency—will probably have differing views on your organizational mission and how and why you serve your clients, students, and patients. We have discussed this challenge in previous chapters, and the means to get everyone on the same page with:

- A mission statement that is current, credible, and can be easily remembered and repeated

- An expression of the mission in policies, programs, and activities

- A strategic plan created by a broad-based planning group that shows your organization's vision for the future and the specific objectives that will help enable the vision

- An internal case statement produced with the input of board and staff members, so that a consensus is reached as to how your organization should be expressed to the community you serve,

THE DEFINITION AND PURPOSE OF MARKETING

Until very recently, the mention of the word "marketing" was nearly anathema in the nonprofit world. Somehow, nonprofits were to be exempt not only from accepted business operating practices, but also free of actively telling their stories in ways that would lead people to their causes. This "purity" was to differentiate the nonprofit world from the perceived-as-tainted profit-making segment of our society. Most nonprofits have learned the lesson that good business practices and honest marketing strategies are necessary to compete in the philanthropic marketplace. Still, there are some few nonprofits that have resisted this trend, lagging behind both in under-standing the importance of marketing, and in creating and implementing effective marketing techniques.

In the first chapter, we discussed the holistic nature of marketing within the larger concept of development. All nonprofit organizations are regularly sending messages to their clients, constituencies, and visitors whether or not there is an intentional effort to "do marketing." From the moment a client, student, patient, or visitor enters the physical environment in which you deliver services and encounter volunteers and staff members, multiple impressions are being made that are both conscious and subconscious. For those who are regularly in contact with your organization, what were once first impressions are either being reinforced or altered in positive and negative ways.

The most profound way to illustrate this concept is to relate a personal experience. Several years ago, my uncle had to have surgery on his heart at a major metropolitan hospital center. The procedure was non-intrusive, and would only require an overnight stay. He and my aunt were nervous about driving through city traffic. They asked if I would take them to the hospital, spend the night at the adjacent hotel, and drive them home the next day. I agreed, but was not looking forward to the encounter with the hospital staff members from experiences at other healthcare institutions. We were all very happily surprised. From the time we arrived through checking out, hospital staff members at every level made generous efforts to accommodate us. Uncle Jim was admitted in a lounge setting with one person sitting with us to make certain everything was in order and to answer our questions. When inquiring about how to get to the hospital hotel, the receptionist called a security officer who drove us to our car, loaded our luggage in his car, drove us to the hotel, and even carried our bags to the room. My uncle not only had successful surgery, but the nurses and orderlies caring for him made his stay as pleasant as a patient's could be. We were so impressed that we complimented a nurse who told us that two short years earlier, our experience would have been different—and not better. At that time, the hospital administrator hired a consultant to assess the hospital's services and make recommendations for improvement. Among the suggested changes, he had apparently recommended that employees be evaluated on their attitudes and method of delivering services. We benefitted from the results.

All who continue to be committed to volunteering and making financial contributions have decided that one or more of their needs are being met by their association with your organization. It is important, then, for each nonprofit to identify the specific spiritual, personal, and community needs that it meets, and to develop the means to remind its supporters of these on a regular basis. It is equally important to create and foster environmental and programmatic "connectors" that will cement their individual decisions to find personal satisfaction by their relationship with your organization.

All marketing plans must begin with the nonprofit's mission, and any plan element must in some fashion help the nonprofit fulfill that statement of its mission. Any marketing message that does not support the mission is false and will not be effective in building a cohesive organization. Once the mission is clear, a listing of the offerings in programs and services is created. Such a list will serve an affirmative purpose, as well as reveal areas where there are opportunities for development. Next, assessing the attitudes, expectations, and ownership of your constituencies and other target audiences enables a clearer, more accurate understanding of whether or not assumptions of attitudes are accurate. This assessment can best be done through a combination of representative interviews and one or more group meetings, so individuals can clarify and articulate the reasons for their involvement. This process will also identify troublesome areas that the leadership can work to improve. Armed with knowledge, a coherent marketing plan can be written and implemented with realistic elements and objectives.

Fundamental to understanding marketing is to recognize that its purpose is to get members of the organization's target audiences to act in one or more ways that will benefit the organization. Communications, then, is an important tool, but when deciding various mediums to use, keep in mind that only telling the story of the nonprofit will not in itself lead individuals to understand how their needs will be met by becoming engaged with your organization. There must be intentionality—and focus—in your messages that will influence or evoke a change in behavior that will benefit your nonprofit.

WHAT'S IN A NAME?

The name by which your organization is known can make a positive, negative, or confusing statement about who you are and whom you serve. Think about the names of nonprofits besides your own and the feelings they invoke. When you do this exercise, you are conducting a bit of market research on yourself about whether or not the name of organization X or Y immediately evokes understanding and appreciation of their mission. In this very basic way, we get a

clearer comprehension of the importance of branding to connecting your organization with the members of your logical target audiences.

Since 1924, the Memorial Child Guidance Clinic delivered mental health
and developmental services to children in greater metropolitan Richmond, Virginia. While the name was not misleading, it did require some explaining to
potential supporters. Then, in 2007, the board of directors accepted a recommendation to change the name to ChildSavers, and the organization's marketing
and fundraising has significantly improved, along with its ability to meet the
needs of more children in distress.

Goodwill Industries offers another variation on this theme. Each local Goodwill operates retail stores that sell donated clothing and other items at discounted
prices as a principal source of funding. Most also operate other businesses from
laundry to custodial services to sheltered workshops that produce income, and
enable Goodwill to provide training and jobs to individuals with varying degrees
of disabilities. Goodwill is all about jobs, but this primary mission is not widely
understood by the public who donate used goods to the nonprofit. Most people
feel good about Goodwill, believe strongly that it is providing help to the less
fortunate, and are happy to be helping it. The name and the brand "Goodwill
Industries" engage the minds and hearts of people all across the country. As a
side note, when individuals learn about what Goodwill is really doing—giving
people with disabilities training and a chance to work—the allegiance to the
nonprofit grows stronger.

Another program that rescues young adults and puts them on a path to
education, employment, and more productive lives, uses basketball as a hook
to get their attention and participation. This program, Richmond Midnight
Basketball League (RMBL), is the most successful such program still operating in the country, shepherding many young people through obtaining G.E.
D.s, helping them get job training, and even earning scholarships to pursue
higher education. Every participant must sign an agreement to stay in the
program, and the organization has a waiting list. The motto: "No work-
shop, no jump shot" summarizes the activity at the half time of every game
where qualified instructors covers topics ranging from moral values to bal-
ancing checkbooks.

RMBL also suffers from a misleading name. There are after-school, evening,
and weekend programs, but no one plays at midnight. Because of the name, the
nonprofit's leadership is constantly explaining that the name does not accurately
describe the program. Finding a better name has been an on again/off again
pursuit for several years.

Changing an organization name—even in circumstances that cry out for it—
can be daunting at best. We can only encourage an honest assessment by your
leadership to determine if your current name helps, confuses, or hurts your

chances of maximum success. After all, your interest should be in meeting your mission, not hanging on to history.

GET TO KNOW YOUR TARGET AUDIENCES

There are more people interested—or who should be interested—in the mission and work of your organization than you likely know. Whether your mailing list is large or small, the efforts to continue to build the numbers of individuals and businesses who could become engaged with your nonprofit if they:

- Understand how their needs are met by your organization's work
- Are provided information about your work in ways that connect with them so that they feel compelled to act on your behalf

The first step in identifying your target audiences is to examine carefully what your organization does that is valuable, and make a precise list. If you have been thorough in drafting the internal case statement, this should be an easy task. Once that is done, distill it to the one or two points that you always want to communicate to any audience. For example, in the for-profit world, GEICO's message is: "Fifteen minutes can save you fifteen percent or more." This is not an easy exercise, but completing it will give you more precision and effectiveness in your messaging. It will also help your organization cut through the noise and clutter of the multi-messages flooding the community from other nonprofits competing for philanthropic support.

In addition to the principal message, there will be other ancillary messages that will be important to individual target audiences. Sometimes, the messages themselves will suggest where to look for the audiences. As an example, if your organization provides free or low-cost day care or pre-school education to the children of the working poor, who benefits from that service? Certainly, parents of your students do. Beyond that group who loves you the most but has little to give financially, employers of the parents have an interest. Those who are concerned about public safety should also be interested, as well as all those who want to give children a chance at a better life through education. The list can continue to build as you think about who the work of your organization touches. Then, the communication pieces, methods, and messages can be tailored to reach individuals in each group.

Remember, you must have a marketing mindset that focuses on what your identified target audience members think and want in order to show them how supporting your nonprofit can satisfy them. Successful marketing is centered on the needs and wants of your target audiences and how your organization is meeting or can meet those needs and wants. Therefore, research and market testing are important to identify correctly the appropriate target audiences and whether or not you are sending them messages to which the members will respond.

When the suggestion of conducting market research is made at many nonprofits—especially ones with small budgets—it is often rejected out of hand. This immediate reaction should not be a surprise, since the accepted wisdom holds that marketing research costs a lot of money. Some techniques utilized by firms that specialize in gathering marketing data will seem expensive; yet, knowing the most effective ways to talk about your organization to the segmented markets will enable more productive results for the financial bottom line.

The fact that your nonprofit cannot afford to hire a firm to conduct marketing research does not obviate the need to know how, what, and to whom you should be telling your organizational story. You cannot be certain that you have successfully crafted your messages, unless you test them with representatives of the target audiences. When properly done, this testing is not only a way to tighten the message and fill in the information gaps. It is also an opportunity to build awareness and a list of significant others who may be interested in your organization.

There are ways to get the marketing data you need without hiring outside help, but it means engaging board members, key volunteers, and staff members in the effort. It is our opinion that using your own internal human resources in market testing can produce the best results; both in gaining knowledge of your constituents and building cohesion and enthusiasm among your organization's leadership.

GETTING THE WORD OUT

Once you have crafted the core messages that you want to instill in the minds of the general public and, in particular, your target audiences, the next task is to determine the delivery methods. The limitation imposed by your budget will expand or shrink your plans, but not necessarily your effectiveness. Paid advertising, for example, is one way to promote your nonprofit, but it is not usually the best. However, if you choose to advertise, be realistic about the objectives you want to achieve. Usually, advertising can only get attention and begin to fuel some interest, but will not be useful in stimulating action.

Some awareness advertising can be obtained through public service spots or by getting a business supporter to underwrite the cost. An especially effective series of ads are the "info ad" variety that enables your organization to give the public information about some aspect of the issues with which you deal and provide statistics and other facts that will both educate and enable your organization to be thought of having expertise in the field.

Making use of your local media—print, radio, and TV—should be a part of the mix of telling your story. The old standby press release remains valuable, but there are three factors that will assist you in actually getting some form of it in the press and broadcast media: 1) know the media's preferred means of receiving the release; 2) learn the best day of the week to send the release; and 3) make the substance of the release newsworthy.

The care and feeding of the reporters who are responsible for covering the nonprofit community is strategic to getting the stories you actually want covered in print or on the air. Get to know each of them, take them a press kit, ask them what they want, and then give it to them in the format they have requested. The best coverage often comes from suggested stories that the reporters write themselves, so give them some ideas to consider. Do not be afraid to be creative in building relationships and getting the attention of the press. A colleague, Pat Morris, when she was Vice President of Philanthropy for the Central Virginia Foodbank, once filled toy trucks with "dump cake" and took them to local reporters.

There will be opportunities to invite the print and broadcast media to cover an event where news will be made. These take the forms of press conferences, groundbreakings, ribbon-cuttings, dedication ceremonies, volunteer work days, and others. Visuals should always be considered a priority when setting up the event. TV reporters will, quite naturally, appreciate having something interesting to film, but even print reporters use photographs. In every case, the most interesting story and visuals get used unless your event occurs on a very slow news day.

We are fully immersed in the electronic pool—websites, e-mail, Facebook, Twitter, and blogging all offer cost-effective ways to tell your story—and all should be considered. However, it remains important to use only those methods that you can do well and to wait on those others with which you do not have the time and knowledge to use effectively. As an example, blogging is a full-contact activity so that regular attention must be given to generating material and responding to comments. Facebook and Twitter have their uses, but they can also be clutter for friends and followers if too much information is shared too often.

Of primary importance is having and maintaining a good website that is attractive and easy to navigate. We are not website designers, but there are many designers in the marketplace who offer their services at affordable rates. We can advise that you must be responsible for keeping the information accurate and current. Nothing can turn off a surfer to your site more quickly than your obvious lack of attention to the contents. If you have a calendar, for instance, make certain it is up-to-date. Websites can also make it convenient for individuals to give financially, and that is one feature you should never be without. More and more, the under 40 generations are using the web to give to charities.

Newsletters—whether e-newsletters or hard copy—give you 100 percent control of your message and allow you to highlight the achievements and the people important to delivering your services. This is a good place to emphasize that every publication and every communication should have as its ultimate goal that of influencing positive movement of your target audiences toward better understanding, appreciation, and support of your organization.

USING YOUR AVAILABLE HUMAN RESOURCES

Assessing the current perception of your organization and its ability to broaden its appeal and support should be an active part of your marketing and communications efforts. Some nonprofits use a firm that specializes in conducting such studies; however, most organizations are unable to afford using outside marketing professionals. It is our experience that this assessment can be done using the staff and volunteers available to you. Lack of money should not deter effective external analysis of your organization's image, brand, and messages, nor its aim to influence the behavior of individuals to select your organization as one to support.

One of the first tasks to complete in preparing to conduct an assessment activity is the creation of a presentation from the internal case statement. Often PowerPoint works quite well, enabling information to be combined with images to help bring your organization's mission and work to life when you make the presentation. Once this has been done, you are ready to conduct a program to strengthen your case for support, effectively inform suspects and prospects, and identify other individuals who could become important advocates and donors.

Personal contact with a board member or key staff member, either one-on-one or in a group setting, will often produce better results than an outside person, and you get the additional benefit of beginning to build a relationship directly with members of your target audiences. Board members, in particular, can be especially helpful in developing lists of suspects and prospects, and giving information that will assist in building profiles of these individuals. Volunteers can be organized into ad hoc committees to do telephone surveys to gather data and test marketing messages. We will address the necessity of using volunteers in a later chapter, but they should always be considered a central resource to use in learning how your organization is perceived and in broadening the ownership of your organization and its mission.

There is an effective, formalized program to use staff and willing board members in a non-threatening way, to tell your story to a broader audience. Known as the Prospect Identification Program, it enables your organization to "do marketing" one-on-one with those whom you need to be informed, and gather names of others to whom your story should be told. This program will be discussed in greater detail in Chapter 6 because its principal purpose is identifying major gift prospects. However, use of this program illustrates the interrelationship of the components of successful development.

Some organizations have been successful in using a local, regional, or national celebrity spokesperson in getting out their message. You could probably name a few of the celebrities you have seen on TV who have been creating awareness and asking support of causes, ranging from feeding starving children to curing breast cancer. Celebrities can, indeed, change minds and give a higher profile to the organizations they are representing. If you are considering using a celebrity to advance your cause, exercise some degree of caution. When a celebrity becomes associated with your nonprofit, you become associated with the celebrity and his or her public behaviors. Even celebrities considered "safe" have disappointed, as the daily headlines will attest. The message here is not to deny yourself this possibility, but to be very careful.

WRITING THE MARKETING AND COMMUNICATIONS ACTION

As with other action-oriented plans, the marketing and communications plan should be specific about what you want to accomplish within the fiscal year. Armed with the information, language, and objectives contained in the strategic plan, expressed in the internal case statement and the information collected through prospect interviews, you should:

- List the human and written resources that are available to you to tell the organization's story accurately.
- List the groups to whom the story should be told.
- Select the key messages—expressed in simple sentences—that should be communicated. These messages should do two things: emphasize strengths and correct misconceptions, if any.

You are now ready to determine what actions will be included in your plan that will help tell your organization's story to the previously identified target audiences. The following are suggested elements for you to consider:

- Regular communication with those on your mailing list. These can take many forms and, with e-newsletters, you can be in touch with members of your target audiences with messages that will be important and encouraging to each of them. It is still recommended that you create or continue a regularly (quarterly) issued newsletter or magazine that provides the unifying and "big picture" view of your organization. Use caution, as well, with older members of your constituency who may not be comfortable getting information by computer.

- An Annual Report and Honor Roll of Donors that gives an accurate report to your constituents and to society of what you have accomplished, who was important to your ability to serve, and the financial status of your organization.

- Special "insider" letters can be used effectively with major prospects/donors to give them information that is not being widely disseminated. A president's or CEO's letter is the most typical of this type in which he or she can give a more personal view of the organization, its challenges, and express appreciation to the recipients for their continuing involvement. Most will even include the lighter moments in leading the organization.

- Personal visits with the reporters/editors who are assigned to your "beat." Building a relationship with them will help you and them do a better job. Take them a press kit, learn what information they want, how they want it, and what day is best to receive it. Cultivating this relationship will pay dividends in getting better coverage of your organization.

- Brochures and other materials for general and target audiences, created with the input of others on the development staff.

- A speakers' bureau using the CEO, other staff members, and willing board members. The brochure for this service should include topics as well as the speakers and their bios. Rotary, Kiwanis, and other service clubs have many programs to fill during the year and have members who could become your supporters.

- Visits at your facilities, if your program is one that can be observed in operation. Some of the best are hosted by individual board members who invite their friends and colleagues to come and learn about their nonprofit. These can range from having lunch with the children at pre-school to observing the program providing work to the disabled.

- Audiovisual materials for use in giving speeches, making presentations, and sending to constituents. Caution is urged because too much money has been wasted by organizations believing that video production was needed without thinking about how and why it would be used.

- A communications/marketing advisory committee comprised of professionals in writing, design, marketing, broadcasting, etc. This committee can be useful in reviewing and making recommendations on the design and content of marketing materials. Members who are working in marketing and communications also give you and your organization access to their companies.

Your plan should be specific about the objectives you will work to accomplish, and include the action steps (with deadlines) to achieve each one.

INTERNAL MARKETING AND COMMUNICATIONS

The words of an old song say it best: "You always hurt the ones you love, the ones you shouldn't hurt at all."

Of all the avoidable errors consistently made, that of taking your organization's internal constituency for granted tops the list. CEOs and other leadership often become so involved in running their organizations, building relationships with major prospects, creating plans for the strengthening/expanding of the program, and so on, that they forget to talk about what is going on and why to their staff members. Then, they are surprised by low morale, lack of support, and, sometimes, bitterness within the ranks.

We do not know the status of the internal communications at your organization, but we do suggest that you take some time to review the matter. Some questions you may ask are:

- Do you have a regular newsletter that keeps the staff up to date?
- Are there mechanisms in place for staff members to participate in reviews of the programs and policies within their areas of work and expertise?
- Are staff members asked what they need to do their jobs or are plans made without their input?
- Are staff members used in creating and making the case for support?
- Are reports made to staff members indicating how the development program has/will affect their programs and activities?
- Are staff members made to feel, in a variety of ways, that they are the reason for the organization's good reputation and success?

We have made the point elsewhere that marketing includes everyone associated with your organization. Spending time cultivating and building good relationships with your internal constituency will give you the solid base needed for a productive program to raise friends and funds.

BEING PREPARED FOR CRISIS MANAGEMENT

A plane carrying the entire men's basketball team and coaches has crashed on its way back from a holiday tournament. A fifth-grade teacher at the local elementary school has been arrested on charges of child molestation. A raging fire in the college dormitory has taken the lives of three students while destroying a major facility. All of these situations and more are examples of the crises—sudden, unpleasant, and sometimes painfully tragic—that overcome everything else that yesterday seemed so important.

Crises are unpredictable, jarring events that can unnerve the most stolid of nonprofit CEOs, board, and staff members. Having a crisis management plan in place before an embarrassing or tragic event will help prevent immobilization and the making of mistakes that could adversely affect your organization for years to come. The crisis management plan is a public relations insurance policy that, unfortunately, too few nonprofits have.

For a crisis management plan to be adopted and accepted, it should fit your organization's culture. However, all such plans have certain elements in common:

- Identification of the types of crises that will trigger the plan
- An established chain of command with phone numbers
- An identified crisis management team and a spokesperson to whom all media will be referred
- A prearranged crisis center to accommodate press, rescue workers, and necessary staff members
- A notification process of key staff members and the organization's community
- A process to prepare official fact sheets/press releases

At all times, but especially in a crisis, honesty must be maintained in statements made to your internal constituency and the media. You want your organization to move forward after the crisis has passed and to be seen in all ways to operate with the highest degree of integrity. You must think beyond the moment to the long-term health of your organization. Through the crisis and after, your aim should be to retain/gain respect and receive the best treatment possible from print and broadcast media. Make time to evaluate as you live through the crisis and in the aftermath, so that your organization's leadership has the ability to develop strategies for the recovery period.

Any crisis management plan must be reviewed critically by appropriate staff members and approved by the board. Then, the plan should be rehearsed and reviewed on an annual basis. With luck, your organization will never need to implement your plan—but it is wise to be prepared.

In Summary

Money can be effectively raised only by helping your target audiences understand, accept, and appreciate how your nonprofit meets one or more of their needs. Those needs will vary from person to person, but the missions of nonprofits generally touch emotions as much or more as they do the intellect. An old but true saying is that people give to people. Define the issues that your organizations address, determine who makes up your target audiences, research thoroughly to the extent possible, and create and test your messages. But, always remember that while marketing programs should use all available means to broadcast the organizations' story, the messages themselves are the keys to capturing the attention and the support of your potential donors.

MARKETING/ COMMUNICATIONS ADVISORY COMMITTEE JOB DESCRIPTION

Overview

The role of the marketing/communications committee is to promote understanding, appreciation, and confidence of (alumni(ae), parents, grandparents, prospective students and their parents, business leaders, members of a related religious denomination, and the various other publics of the local community) in (Name of Organization). The committee's work is focused on helping tell the organization's story accurately and effectively using appropriate communication tools. Assessing the public's perception of the organization and its work will be an important component of its charge.

Functions of the Marketing/Communications Committee

- Make recommendations concerning programs and activities that will increase the acceptance, confidence, involvement, and support of (Name of Organization) in its activities locally, regionally, and nationally.
- Recommend to the organization's top officials and to volunteer leaders of the development program what must be done to assure understanding on the part of its key publics.
- Study and analyze ways by which the organization relates to its publics and recommend ways the organization can improve these efforts.

- Help the officials of (Name of Organization) better to understand the needs of the markets served by the organization, and to assess current perceptions of (focus of activity) in general and (Name of Organization) specifically.

- Conduct a periodic review of the organization's processes and methods of communication with its key public, and with staff and constituents being served.

Emphases for the Communications/Marketing Committee Should Be to:

- Focus on the central role of (primary organizational focus/mission) — the benefits to (those served, community, etc.). Show the impact of the organization throughout the community and beyond.

- Call attention to the values of the work of the organization. Show that the work of the organzation is second to none. Emphasize the special qualities and strengths of (Name of Organization).

- Determine the cost/benefit ratio to the community and see why the organization is worth the investment.

SAMPLE MARKETING INTERVIEW QUESTIONS

1. What do you understand is the mission and purpose of the organization?

2. Why do you believe the organization is important?

3. What do you think is the perception of the organization in your circles? In the community?

4. How would you rate the organization's communications program (scale of 1–10)? What do you recall as the last message in the media/mail/etc. concerning the organization?

5. What type of communication would you like to receive from the organization?
   a. _____Quarterly newsletter or magazine
   b. _____E-mail newsletter or bulletins
   c. _____Website newsletter
   d. _____USPS for special events/activities
   e. _____Newspaper (press releases, paid advertising)
   f. _____Radio, TV
   g. _____Other

6. How often do you think the organization should be communicating with the community?

7. What are the strengths of the organization?

8. What are its weaknesses?

9. How would you rate the organization in each of the following?

	Exc.	Good	Avg	Fair	Poor
Administration					
Staff					
Financial Management					
Communications					
Public Relations/Outreach					

10. How would you rate the organization's programs?

	Exc.	Good	Avg	Fair	Poor
(List of Programs)					

11. What other programs would you like to see the organization create?

12. Have you ever visited the organization? If so, what was your overall impression?

13. What do you think is the foremost reason people give to/volunteer for the organization?

14. What are your current philanthropic priorities?

15. Knowing what you now know about the organization, what, in your opinion, is the single most important message that the organization should communicate to the communities it serves?

16. Now that we have had this conversation, would you be more or less willing to contribute financially to the organization if you were asked?

17. Are there others in your community that you believe would be interested in knowing more about the organization?

18. Is there anything else you would like for me to know that I have not asked?

SAMPLE MARKETING/ COMMUNICATIONS PLAN

Mission Statement

The mission of (Name of Organization)'s communications effort is to increase the public understanding, acceptance, and appreciation of the organization.

Keys to Effective Communications

Effective communications programs succeed when each staff member and volunteer realizes that public relations is everyone's job.

A positive attitude about our organization's mission, history, and present contributions to the public is critical for success.

Remember that people are not generally interested in our organization's needs, our interests. They want to know how we meet the public's needs, the public's goals, and the public's interests.

Success is important. People back winners. But, portray successes in terms of service.

The most effective communications is person to person.

Meeting the Challenge

The (Name of Organization)'s communications program must accomplish:

1. Greater understanding and appreciation of (Name of Organization) throughout the service area:
    a. Increased involvement in the support of the organization by community leaders
    b. Increased publicity concerning the impact of the organization on the lives of the citizens in the service area
    c. Increased understanding of the financial benefit to citizens afforded by the operation of the organization
    d. Increased reliance on the leadership of the organization as expert resources in matters relating its expertise

2. Greater financial support from persons, organizations, and businesses in the service area for capital and annual needs:
    a. Increased information on who should and could be supporting the organization
    b. Increased information from the organization on how donated funds are used

Plan Elements and Action Steps

1. Case Statement
    a. Complete the internal case statement
    b. Secure board approval
    c. Develop/produce external materials
        i. Executive summary for market-testing and to accompany proposals for major gifts
        ii. Campaign brochure for major prospects
        iii. Abbreviated brochure for larger prospect pool
        iv. Information brochure on (Name of Organization) that incorporates case language, etc.
        v. "Flip Chart" presentation for individual presentations
        vi. PowerPoint presentation
        vii. Multi-media presentation

2. Communications and Events Committee—This committee is responsible for planning and implementing activities that will enable better understanding, acceptance, and appreciation for (Name of Organization) and the campaign goals. Activities may include:
   a. Developing and overseeing the implementation of a communications/marketing plan for (Name of Organization)
   Facilitating small group gatherings for pace-setting and major gift prospects—individual and corporate
   b. Assisting in the development of materials for the public relations program for (Name of Organization) and for the campaign, specifically
   c. Issuing appropriate press releases on (Name of Organization), campaign leadership, and progress
   d. Planning and implementing the public announcement
   The committee should be chaired by a member of board of (Name of Organization) and include non–board members who have interests and skills in various aspects of the communications arts and event planning. The committee should call upon each board and staff member to assist in telling the story of the organization as may be appropriate. The chair of this committee should become a member of the campaign steering committee when it is constituted.

3. Print and Broadcast Media
   a. Write/send bi-weekly press releases on (Name of Organization) activities, new member, new board members, and any other human interest/community interest story.
   b. Develop a press kit.
   c. Build a list of key reporters at local papers and other media outlets
   d. Use board members to arrange appointments with these reporters to inform them of the work of (Name of Organization).
   e. Shop potential feature stories with these key reporters.
   f. Invite reporters to cover events and activities at the organization and other locations.
   g. Place monthly "info ads" in selected newspapers that speak to the organization's field of expertise, organization history and accomplishments, etc. Get ads underwritten by one or more businesses.
   h. Organize individuals to write letters to the editor, expressing appreciation for the work of the organization, etc.
   i. Attempt to have the president be a guest on a call-in radio program.

4. Civic and Professional Groups
   a. Draft a basic speech on the organization for volunteers to use as a basis for making a presentation. Speech draft must contain key "talking points" that every presentation should include.
   b. Select prominent civic/business clubs to provide informational program on the organization and the private/public partnership.
   c. Select other key groups and/or associations for similar programs.

    d. Present program to chamber of commerce board on (Name of Organization).

5. Public Forums/Displays
   a. Set up in mall—empty store would provide best opportunity, but a booth would do if other not possible. Dispense information, do demonstrations, etc., as space and management allow.
   b. Use events already scheduled to provide information to citizens about the role and importance of the (Name of Organization).
   c. Provide educational programs in schools to classes or assemblies.

6. Individual Meetings and Small Group Gatherings
   a. These gatherings are held with major corporate and/or individual prospects to test reaction to the case and build interest and ownership of the campaign goals. A volunteer who extends the invitations to his/her friends hosts the gatherings.
   b. Individual test-marketing sessions can be scheduled with the consultant or the organization's president.

7. Publications/Other Media
   a. Use an informational newsletter/magazine as a means of providing information about the organization's work to constituents.
   b. A special "insiders" letter from the president of the organization to major prospects, major donors, key political persons, etc.
   c. An Annual Report and Honor Roll of Donors should be published after the current fiscal year.
   d. A calendar and/or other image-enhancing publications may be considered.
   e. Remember the direct mail appeals are direct marketing opportunities and should be created with this in mind.

CHAPTER 6

The Fundraising Program

There is an old story about a man discovering another man searching the ground around a streetlight on a moonless night. The first man asked what the second was searching for and if he could be of assistance. The second man replied that he lost a valuable ring and was grateful for the offer of help.

After some time had gone by without finding the ring, the first man wondered why they were having such trouble. Finally, he inquired of the second man exactly where he was walking or standing when the ring was lost. The second man pointed to a hedge ten feet away. "Why," the first man exclaimed, "are we looking for it here?!" "The light is better," explained the second man.

Before you are too critical of the man who lost the ring, you must admit that all of us tend to do the comfortable thing, if we can, rather than tackle what appears to be difficult. You, too, can be guilty of "searching in the light" instead of planning as carefully as possible to find and obtain the friends and funds your organizations require. When you do not have a written plan to keep you focused on productive activity, you will tend to spend time and energy in comfortable pursuits, whether or not they are helping you achieve your goals.

Writing a plan about how you *should* be spending your time and your organization's resources often seems more difficult than just "doing the job." In fact, a common excuse is: "I'm too busy. I don't have time to plan." Time is a precious commodity to any development officer. Therefore, the majority of your time should be spent wisely in those activities that will produce the best possible results. The only way you can be certain that this will happen is to have a well thought-out written plan of action—and implement it.

PLANNING TO SUCCEED

All planning processes have similar components, whether you are preparing a strategic plan or an annual action plan for development.

- **Mission.** Everything that you do or plan to do on behalf of your organization must flow from an understanding of who you are and whom you serve. In addition, you and other members of your staff should write a development program mission statement. Both should appear at the beginning of the plan.

- **The Current Status.** In order to determine what must be accomplished in the coming year, you need to know where you stand at the present. Gather as much current data from reports and development staff discussions as you can. Also, interview other key staff, trustee leadership, and select volunteers to get their views on what was done well and how things might be done better.

- **Charting the Course.** Following the honest analysis, the objectives to be accomplished within the coming year can be set. Some of the objectives will be arbitrary because of organizational planning that has already been approved by the board. Other objectives will have been determined by the demands of the operating budget, or the plant emergencies that cannot be covered by current resources. Last, there should be objectives that will relate directly to strengthening your department's ability to serve the organization, including challenging staff members to become increasingly more knowledgeable and effective.

- **Assessing Progress and Making Corrections.** After the creation of any plan, there will be information and impediments that could not have been anticipated. Constant monitoring of the implementation of the plan and a willingness to make course corrections are essential to success.

Asking and answering the following questions can make your planning activity more targeted and effective:

- Is the organizational case statement adequate and up to date?

- What annual fundraising goals were attempted last year, and were they achieved?

- How were the fundraising goals set, and was the process effective?

- If you are in a capital effort, what specific goals must be accomplished in the upcoming fiscal year?

- What pieces of printed material are being used, and for what purposes?

- Who is currently involved in telling the story of your organization (CEO, other staff members, board members, alumni, physicians, etc.) and how successful have they been?

- How has the CEO been involved and has this been a productive use of his/ her time and energy?

- Is the current system of recordkeeping and response to donors up to expectations? Can you get the reports you need to do your work efficiently?

- How are volunteers being utilized in both program and fundraising activities?

- What is the status of the internal operation of the development office?

- Are there relationship issues within the department/organization that have an impact on your ability to function effectively?

Okay, you say, you may know more than you wanted to about the development program, its needs, and the human factors that will have an impact on its progress. How do you translate that pile of information into a workable action plan?

As we learned earlier in this book, the function of development can be summarized into two primary goals—marketing/communications and fundraising. The most successful planning template, then, is one that organizes the objectives you wish to accomplish under one of these two overriding functions. Those activities that are primarily relationship-building, informing to increase understanding, and creating greater appreciation for the services your organization provides to meet the needs of society, and, thereby, to influence or change the behavior of your target audiences toward supporting your organization, should be listed under the marketing/communications function. Those that are principally related to the raising of money should be grouped under the fundraising function. Of course, the two functions are interrelated, but this approach may help you and your staff members more clearly articulate your annual objectives.

For any plan to be accepted and effective, stakeholders must have had an opportunity for input and—whenever possible—to have had a substantive role in creating that portion which they must implement. This includes support staff members who are responsible for preparing mailings, providing lists, arranging meetings—doing all of the support work that enables the CEO, board members, and development officers to work more efficiently. It is wise to listen to those who perform the work. Because they are involved daily, they can, and do, offer good advice on how to accomplish the many nitty-gritty, necessary, unglamorous tasks that are the base of every development program. These tasks range from preparing and sending invitations for special events, to printing and sending fundraising letters. When they are included they have ownership of the plan and, as an added bonus, will make certain that conflicts in scheduling are avoided.

Here are the steps recommended to make certain that everyone is involved and acquires ownership of the annual development plan.

Step 1. Schedule a planning session for your staff members at a location where telephones are hard to find and cell phones are prohibited (except during breaks). If you can, take them to a retreat location.

Step 2. Make a presentation, lead a discussion, and answer questions on the overall organizational objectives that the department must help accomplish. Invite the CEO and the board development chair to participate in this part of the meeting.

Step 3. Ask each staff member to make a presentation to the group on his/her area of responsibility, including what was accomplished the previous year and the proposed plan for the coming year. Each objective should have action steps and specific target dates for completion.

Step 4. Show the interrelationships that exist between the individual areas of responsibility; lead a thorough discussion of each presentation.

Step 5. Be aware of how any new program or expansion of a present program affects the department's budget. Determine if a request for additional funds or a readjustment of budgeted funds will be necessary.

Step 6. With support staff present, transfer the elements of the plan that make an impact on the office work schedule (direct mail, magazine, newsletters, etc.) to a master calendar. *Listen* to your support staff and make adjustments as may be required.

Step 7. Present the plan to the CEO for review and comment. It is important that his/her priorities are reflected in the plan for it to be accepted and successful.

Step 8. Present the completed plan to the development committee of the board for its review and acceptance.

Step 9. In conjunction with the development chair of the board, distribute the plan and make a presentation to the full board, and ask for the board's acceptance and support.

Step 10. Following the board's understanding and acceptance of the annual development action plan, it is approved and implemented.

We realize that not every chief development officer has a staff, and many of our readers are responsible for the full program with very little office support personnel. Yet, the process is valid regardless of the number of persons involved. The key is to build a logical, workable plan on paper, and get the ownership and participation of those persons you need to accomplish your goals.

THE ANNUAL FUND—ACQUIRING, KEEPING, AND GROWING DONORS

From the time when we were children, we heard the parable of the two men who built houses on very different foundations. The first valued beachfront property and constructed his house right on the sand where he would have a great view of the sea in all of its moods. Unfortunately for him, the sea has a nasty temper at times, and the first man's house was washed away.

The second man also enjoyed the ocean, but he was more prudent about his choice of locations. He built his home on solid rock, and, the story goes, survived the severest storms in relative safety. He may have even added another floor.

The point, of course, is that wise people make certain that lives, as well as houses, are built on solid principles—that they are well-founded—so that they will be buttressed against the inevitable storms that all of us must weather.

Development programs, too, must be carefully built on a solid foundation. For development, the firm foundation is the Annual Fund. Without a solid basis of support from a cross-section of your constituency, there is no real way for your program consistently to secure larger gifts for capital or special purposes or to build an adequate endowment. While there may be the significant single major gift from time to time, these will be the exceptions and will not be sufficient to accomplish your organizational objectives.

There are six main functions of every Annual Fund. They are:

1. Raising the funds your organization needs for its operating budget and, if possible, additional dollars for discretionary use (debt retirement, equipment purchase, endowment, etc.).

2. Telling the organization's story on a regular basis to every member of your constituency (direct marketing).

3. Acquiring the first gift from a brand new donor.

4. Enabling the process of establishing and building a relationship with each donor so that they will better understand the importance of their support and keep giving.

5. Providing the possibility of moving the donor into a willingness to reach his or her highest annual giving potential.

6. Providing the pool of potential major gift and planned gift prospects for inclusion in your major prospects management program.

Basic Steps to Building a Healthy and Productive Annual Fund

Since the Annual Fund is the foundation upon which your development program is built, it is wise to make certain that all of the steps necessary for success are taken—that no corners are cut. If you have an Annual Fund program, but are concerned about its productivity, the following steps are offered to help you examine your process and give you ideas for strengthening your efforts.

- *Assign the right staff member.* Though it sounds so fundamental, make certain that responsibility for the Annual Fund has been assigned to one staff member and that he or she has been given the training, time, and budget necessary to do the job. Do not underestimate the knowledge and skills that a development professional needs to engender annual support for your organization, especially the ability to work with a cadre of volunteers.

- *Write an Annual Fund Case Statement.* Most development officers confront the case statement only when their institutions are preparing to conduct a capital campaign. Even then, it is often an incomplete document written mostly for external consumption as a campaign marketing piece. Rarely does anyone think of the need to be thorough about answering the questions beyond why you need the annual dollars, but why members of your target audiences should care enough to send donations to your organization. The case statement for the Annual Fund should not be lengthy, but it should be a well-thought-out document that accomplishes the following:
  - It should clearly state the mission of the organization, who it serves, and why its work is important to the reader.
  - It should establish the place of the Annual Fund in helping to accomplish the mission.
  - It should help to build consensus among the staff, volunteers, and individuals who will be working and/or benefiting from the Annual Fund support.
  - It should provide the basis in reasoning and language for the appeal letters and other material that may be used to solicit contributions. The messages should be both consistent and compelling.

- *Identify and recruit an Annual Fund Committee.* It is important to carefully identify and recruit individuals to serve on an Annual Fund Committee as for any other group of fundraising volunteers, offering an important opportunity to bring new people and energy to your organization. It is recommended that the committee membership represent the target audiences who will be solicited. There is no substitute for peer-to-peer appeals, whether it is in person or by letter. Therefore, select and invite the best prospective committee members who are within your nonprofit's reach. The committee should also include the board member who will have the task of soliciting fellow board members.

- As with any other volunteer committee, prepare a job description that comprehensively outlines the volunteer's role as a member of the group. Make certain, too, that the volunteer knows the expectation of being a donor to the Annual Fund at a level appropriate to his/her leadership and ability. Do not assume that the prospective volunteer will understand this requirement when being recruited. An important rule when dealing with volunteers is to be absolutely honest about expectations before the individual agrees to become involved.

- The first recruit for the Annual Fund Committee is the chair. Often, the chair can be a member of the board; however, whoever is chosen should be one who can both raise money and help recruit effective members of the committee.

- *Set measureable goals.* These should include participation as well as dollar goals and can be divided by constituent group (alumni, patients, etc.). The goals must always address the basic annual needs of your organization, but they should be measured, as well, against last year's real figures. It is a good idea for your monthly reports on progress to show comparative figures from the previous year at the same point in time. This helps to motivate and give greater focus to the volunteers who are instrumental in your ability to be successful.

- *Write a plan of action.* The plan for your Annual Fund program should include details and deadlines of the tasks to be completed for the fiscal year—meetings of the Annual Fund Committee, number and dates of direct mail appeals, periods for one-on-one solicitations for special gifts, etc. The plan should be reviewed by the Annual Fund Committee and, after editing, be approved by the group. As much as possible, the committee members need to own the plan that they will play an essential part of implementing.

- *Determine the number and kind of printed materials needed to promote the Annual Fund.* Usually, a brochure is created and printed that can be mailed along with an appeal letter or handed to a prospect when a personal call is made by a volunteer. Depending on your needs and creativity, you may require invitations for special giving levels, postcards, membership cards, and other possibilities to solicit and express appreciation for responses. As much as possible, try to anticipate through planning what will be needed so that you can prepare a realistic budget.

- *Include recognition clubs and societies in your Annual Fund plan.* Recognition clubs/societies have been effective mechanisms to secure, maintain, and increase special annual gifts from individuals and business. Further, these programs help build the relationships between donors and the organization that often lead to successful solicitation of major gifts for capital purposes.

  The typical starting point for club recognition is the $100 level with stair step increases from there. It is recommended the club level increments be set to give donors a realistic possibility of moving up the recognition stairs. For example, it would be easier to ask a $100 donor to move to the $250 club level than to the $500 level.

  Every Annual Fund Recognition program should have a special recognition society for giving $1,000 to $5,000 or more. The top group should reflect your organization's current giving program and experience, but without a specified special recognition for larger gifts, it will be more difficult to encourage donors to participate at the higher levels of annual giving.

  This special recognition group also requires different printed materials and letters of invitation than those used for other levels of solicitation. In some cases, a type of formal invitation is used, sent by a peer, with a follow-up phone call or visit. Whatever is done should be appropriate to your organization, but your approach should be thought of as a major gift process than a typical annual solicitation.

- *Understand that the direct mail solicitations will occur at regular, strategic times during the fiscal year.* This is a complete annual program, not a one-time effort. Each direct mailing is designed to build upon the last, carrying the same messages, but framed in different ways, and sent at times during the year that will help garner positive responses.

Remember that the Annual Fund has a significant role to play in communicating the mission, purpose, and goals of your nonprofit. Therefore, the messages that are conveyed through your case statement, letters, brochures, and personal contact must show how the Annual Fund objectives are in support of those overall organizational goals. In this way, every annual donor, however large or small the gift, can understand and appreciate that he or she has participated in strengthening your program and facilities.

Creating an Effective Direct Mail Solicitation Program

An Annual Fund direct mail program, when properly conceived and implemented, can be one of your most productive ways to raise annual dollars, make new friends, and build closer relationships with your constituents. It is a relatively inexpensive way continually to give consistent reasons why the existence of your organization is important to your targeted audiences and provide a convenient means for them to respond.

The role of direct mail in the development of funds and friends has not always been properly understood or appreciated. Some organizations have been reluctant to use regular direct mail for a number of reasons, among them:

- Fear of alienating constituents by mailing requests to them on a regular basis
- Lack of knowing how to set up and run the program
- Expense of mailing against the expected return
- Bad experience with a past mail campaign
- Board and staff aversion to the receipt of direct mail

While the preceding reasons (or excuses) may be barriers in some organizations to using direct mail, there is overwhelming evidence from nonprofits that use the technique that it produces results both from marketing and fundraising standpoints. If your nonprofit's leadership seems reluctant or resistant to direct mail, conduct research on a few comparable organizations in your area that are using the method. Prepare a report that graphically shows their experiences, and you will likely overcome any objections.

As said above, using direct mail must be considered a complete program that is designed to capture attention, make the case for support, show how the nonprofit meets the recipient's needs, ask for the gift, and provide a convenient way for the donor to respond. This is done over the course of the fiscal year and at times when the recipient will pay attention. Nonprofits that have a July-to-June fiscal year have an advantage in scheduling because they are able to take advantage of two year-ends—December (end of tax year) and June (end of fiscal year). They also do not have the unfortunate problem of those that use a calendar year of wondering when to launch the Annual Fund. January and February are rivaled only by July and August as the worst months in which to ask for money.

Therefore, it is recommended that your program schedule five direct-mail solicitations as follow:

1. September—The "kickoff" mailing containing a letter signed by the appropriate volunteer, a brochure, and a response envelope. Each letter should contain a specific "ask" amount, depending on the experience with the target audience member. Acquisition letters will likely have the same dollar request ($25, $50), while past donors will be asked for a repeat gift or an increased amount. It is never a good idea to give a range or simply ask for any amount. It is important to tell the prospective donor

what you want him or her to consider donating. This is, of course, especially true when asking consideration of a gift that would recognize a donor in a giving club or society.

2. Very Early December—This mailing is comprised of a letter noting the time of the year (Christmas, end-of-tax-year) and may be signed by the chair of the Annual Fund Committee rather than each individual member of the committee.

3. Late March or Early April—A follow-up letter to each of those who have not responded is sent from the Annual Fund Committee member who originally wrote to them giving an update on the progress toward the goal, information about how annual support has been used, and asking again for consideration of the specific gift that was requested in the first letter.

4. May—A "proof sheet" mailing should be sent to everyone on your mailing list. This is not a personal appeal, but tells the donor or prospect that your nonprofit is beginning the preparation for the Annual Report and Honor Roll of Donors. There is a list of donors as of a particular date included with the letter that asks the recipients if their names are spelled correctly and, if a school, if they are listed in the right class. The letter goes on to inform the recipients that it is not too late to make a gift to be included in this year's Honor Roll. This purposefully impersonal mailing reaps considerable results, motivating individuals to give because they see friends or competitors listed and current donors to make additional gifts.

5. Early to Mid-June—This mailing is primarily targeted to those who gave the previous year but have not yet given in the current fiscal year. They are know by the acronym LYBUNTS (Last Year But Unfortunately Not This). Sometimes, organizations also send a letter to those who have given at some point in the last few years to encourage them to repeat. These lapsed donors are called SYBUNTS (Some Year But Unfortunately Not This).

A good technique for those letters signed by volunteers is to use their letterhead and envelopes. Sometimes a business owner or corporate executive will provide their business stationery. Most often, a personal letterhead is produced by the nonprofit with the nonprofit's return address. This method helps get the delivery envelope opened, rather than discarded, so that the contents will be read.

Along with using the volunteers' letterhead, a "live" stamp should be used whenever possible. Postage meters may be more convenient, but a real stamp on the envelope gives the mailing more importance, and also increases the chance that it will be opened. Even bulk mailings can be improved by the use of a "live" third-class stamp. In all cases when sending solicitations for giving recognition clubs and societies, a first-class stamp must be used.

The gift return envelope is an extremely important part of the direct mail package and is too often given little thought. We forget that it is this piece of the mailing package that the interested prospective donor will very likely keep while discarding the solicitation letter and brochure. The return envelope (wallet flap type) should continue to carry the message to remind the individual why it was placed in the stack of bills or set aside for consideration later. This envelope also enables your nonprofit to provide the means for the recipient to communicate with your organization. A list of materials that the individual can request, a request for the name of a prospective student, a means to gather additional contact information about the donor—all of these and more possibilities are available to you if you plan and carefully design your response envelope.

Tips on Writing the Solicitation Letter

If you listen to most volunteers—and some executive directors—there is no higher virtue than the perfect one-page solicitation letter. No one, we are told, wants to read very much, and a brief solicitation will have the most appeal. While that sounds good, the truth is that two-page letters can be more effective than the succinct version. A longer letter often signals that the subject is important, and it tends to get more attention than its shorter brother. In writing the letter, regardless of the length, it is wise to use short paragraphs for ease of reading. And, if you can, make certain the first sentence of each paragraph gives the recipient the message you want to convey, even if he or she only skims the letter.

Originally signed letters always make the best statement, though it is not always practical. If the letter is to invite the recipient to become a member of an annual giving recognition club or to move to a more prestigious grouping, then it should be originally signed. Volunteers should be encouraged to write personal notes if the addressee is a friend, business associate, and the like. If the solicitation is the more general (and numerous) type, a printed signature is acceptable. In all cases, the signature should be in blue ink.

Saying Thank You

Saying a proper "thank you" to each donor is a key part of getting a gift next year. Gifts that are large and not so large should be acknowledged by a letter from the appropriate officer of the organization. Though it will vary by organization, typically the CEO signs letters for gifts of $500 or more, and the chief development officer sends thank-you letters to those who donate under that baseline amount. *It is not recommended that a printed card be used regardless of the size of the gift.* To paraphrase Stanislavski, "There are no small donors, just small gifts." Every donor deserves to be treated as a special asset to your organization.

Some organizations enclose a receipt with the letter. Others use the letter itself on the organization's letterhead as both the receipt and thank you. Whatever you use, it is important that the words "No goods nor services were provided as a result of this gift" appear, either on the receipt or in the letter. If this is not the case, then the thank-you letter must indicate what was provided, and how much of the donation may be deducted from taxes.

For larger annual donations ($500, $1000 or more), an additional note from the volunteer solicitor is often effective. Sometimes, if the gift has been directed toward a specific part of the program (scholarship, patient assistance fund, family assistance), the one who is benefiting may be encouraged to send a note of appreciation. Last, the official thank-you letter should be sent promptly. A good rule of thumb is to have the letter in the mail within three days from the receipt of the gift.

RAISING MAJOR GIFTS

The process of identifying, researching, cultivating, and soliciting prospects for major gifts should be an ongoing part of your organization's development program. Whether the need for major funding is building an endowment, renovating a facility, buying needed equipment, or expanding/underwriting your organization's program, it is important in the short and long term to be continually active in the area of major giving. When you are, you help to ensure that your organization will have developed the resources necessary to meet its needs on an uninterrupted basis, have a well-cultivated major prospect base, and build financial stability.

Most organizations have little trouble making a list of those who are both a part of their constituent family and could, if properly motivated, make a significant gift. The process usually breaks down because there are so many names, few staff members, and not enough time to work with each prospect. So, instead of productive work being done, staff members are frozen in place by the sheer size of the task facing them.

The Eye of the Beholder

At a country church in rural Kansas many years ago, a discussion raged at a council meeting that had already worn out most of the congregation. The question that had twisted the membership in knots was whether to replace the current parsonage with a brand-new one or assist the pastor and his family to buy a home of their own.

Just as they were finally reaching a consensus to help the pastor enjoy home ownership, a longtime member of the church rose to her feet. She spoke with passion about the shame she felt that for the first time in its history, her beloved church was about to abandon its sacred obligation to house the minister. She was so convinced of her position that if the congregation would conduct a campaign to raise money for a new parsonage, she promised, on the spot, to give the first $25. We did not learn if her argument carried the day, but we have a hunch the pastor began to build equity in his own home.

While the amount that your organization considers a major gift is apt to exceed the $25 range, thinking that there is a baseline that is common for every nonprofit would be wrong. However, it is especially important that your organization's leadership determine what constitutes a major gift and not leave that decision to individual donors. What is a major gift? A major gift is one that:

- Could not ordinarily be made on an annual basis
- Is normally targeted to a particular physical facility improvement or endowment
- By its size and nature, will substantially move the organization forward toward meeting one or more of its significant goals

The amount will differ from organization to organization, but the bar must be set so that you have a cutoff point as you qualify prospects for your major prospect list. To reach a consensus on the minimum amount that would qualify a person for your major prospect list, there are several factors that will help you determine the "bottom line" dollar amount for your program at this point in time.

- Are you just beginning an organized major gifts effort, or have you had one in place for three or more years?
- What has been the pattern of giving to your nonprofit over the last ten years? What sizes of gifts have you received and how many?
- What are your current needs for major support, and are they well-defined?
- Do your key volunteers understand the need for major support?
- What kind of organization are you (college, school, hospital, social service agency, etc.)?

Despite other factors, it is recommended that your baseline for including a prospect on your major gifts list begin at a minimum of $10,000. For many organizations that have ongoing major gifts programs, the figure will be much higher. However, for nonprofits that are just beginning to be purposeful about acquiring major gifts, keeping the prospect entry-level high enough—yet achievable—is worth the extra time the CEO, the development staff members, and volunteers will be devoting to them.

Finally, the kind of organization you represent and its history of support have created an attitude among your constituents about what size of gift is appropriate. This is the most difficult—and yet most important—obstacle to overcome. Nothing is more effective in moving your constituents' attitudes to higher levels than raising gifts larger than the majority of your supporters think you can—to make it acceptable for others to give in a similar fashion.

There is no "magic bullet" or short-term answer. The key to success is to establish and carry out a solid, systematic program that continually identifies, qualifies, cultivates, and presents major giving opportunities to appropriate members of your constituency.

Create a List of Major Gift Possibilities

In order to raise major dollars, your organization must create a list of those "big ticket" items for which major funding would enable significant progress in meeting your mission. These may be program underwriting, new equipment, new construction and/or renovations, and endowed funds. It is essential, however, that your organization's leadership determines what you need major funding to accomplish: a) interest from a major prospect; b) making certain that the donor does not drive your funding priorities.

The best list of major funding opportunities includes facilities, program, and endowment needs and wants with the amount necessary for a donor to provide a naming gift. It is also helpful if each item on the list has a brief description of what the significant gift would make possible. And, make certain you include a statement of how the gift would be recognized—immediately and long term.

Building Your Prospect List

A good place to begin in your search for prospects is to ask the question: Who cares or who should care whether or not your organization succeeds in meeting its mission of service? Be realistic, however, as you and others add names to the list because it will be tempting to include individuals with money with whom you have no current connection. Bill Gates will appear on many lists as a person who has wealth. He should not be on yours unless you have someone who can connect your organization with him.

Here are some good places to look for names:

- Current board members, former board members, and their widows/widowers
- Descendants of your organization's founder(s) or early major donors
- Volunteers who have shown an active interest in your nonprofit
- Major donors to prior capital campaigns
- Prominent alumni(ae) or members of constituent organizations (parents, grandparents, etc.)
- Family members of recent major donors
- Prominent business leaders who have a relationship with your organization (employers of alumni(ae), benefit from improved community conditions, etc.)
- Neighbors who have reasons to appreciate the work or your nonprofit
- Persons in retirement home and communities (especially for planned giving)
- Members of a related religious denomination
- Faculty, staff, medical personnel
- Persons who have directly benefitted from the work of your organization (grateful patients, parents, etc.)
- Board members and major donors of competing organizations in your area

Once you have built your list and completed a beginning qualification of the gift potential of each person, the logical next step is to research the names, most especially the most promising ones. Whoever said "Knowledge is power" must have been a successful development officer. There are companies, of course, who provide prospect-rating services that are highly accurate—and very expensive to use. For some organizations, these professional services are within their budgets and are cost effective in assessing the potential of their large and geographically diverse constituents. For the majority of nonprofits, however, other effective means of rating prospects must be utilized.

A traditional method of prospect qualification is to recruit a ratings committee whose sole purpose is to review your list of potential major prospects and help you place them in categories of giving potential. The committee members often add the names of other prospects of whom you were not aware.

Another, less traditional method, is to keep with you a list of prospects about whom you want to know more. When meeting one-on-one with individual board members and other knowledgeable volunteers, if there is time, ask them to look at the list and give you what they might know about one or more of them. This kind of impromptu research can be very helpful in gathering important information that will help you work smarter in cultivation activities.

Finding Prospects You Didn't Know You Had A more formalized program both to tell your organization's story and to identify potential prospects for your organization is known as the Prospect Identification Program. This concept, originally introduced to us by Robert Nelson and the late Robert Parrish of Robert E. Nelson and Associates, enables you to utilize your board and other key volunteers in a non-threatening program to uncover the best prospects for your organization within your ability to reach them.

There are some preliminary steps that your organization must have achieved prior to implementing this program:

- Have reached agreement that your mission statement is current, compelling, and memorable
- Have a board-approved list of major funding needs
- Have reached consensus on how your organization will be described through the process of creating an internal case statement
- Have created a presentational version of the case statement that has been adapted to PowerPoint

Once you done these things, then you are ready to go fishing for new prospects.

We are all influenced by the decision-making social systems that surround us and our organizations. Known as power structures, the ability of the organization to be sensitive to, understand, and use their influence will often determine that organization's ultimate success or failure.

Power structures depend on the interactions of persons known as "power players" who have the capacity to control the actions of others through "societal power." Those who exercise societal power may be divided into these broad groupings:

- **Command.** The person controls others because of an elected or appointed office and the power is the same regardless who holds the office.
- **Influence.** The person has facilities or abilities that enables power to be exerted. It may be due to a number of factors (skill in directing others, reciprocal arrangements, special knowledge, reputation, wealth, control of resources).
- **Intimidation** (illegitimate). The person compels others to act against their will.

Though we do not necessarily enjoy thinking in these terms, social power does exist and is employed in every social system. So, it is important for development professionals to understand this truth and realistically make use of methods to discover these power players in order to bring them into a productive relationship with your organizations.

Power players are more likely to use their influence rather than authority that may come from observable positions in community organizations. They have probably been active in formal organizations within the past 5 to 15 years. Generally, power players share the following characteristics:

- They are 50 years of age and older.
- They are in the higher income group in your community.
- They are in positions of control or have access to credit, money, jobs, and media.
- They are above average in formal education within their age group.
- They are normally self-employed, owners, or chief executives.
- They are usually longtime residents of the community.

It is entirely possible that the power player has made no real effort to achieve influence. Yet, because of demonstrated abilities, because of the respect held for them within the community and their peer groups, they are leaders—power players.

Power players or key leaders relate to each other and thereby constitute a power structure. While power structures that exist in your community may have unique characteristics, there are certain basic types that can be listed.

- **Single Individual.** Some communities have a power structure centered in one person. Where this exists, enablers who do his/her bidding surround the "power player." Normally, this occurs in communities that are dominated by one family, one company, or one industry.
- **Single Group.** Some communities have an elite power group that controls policy-making.
- **Power Split.** Examples of such splits are:
  - Republican/Democratic
  - Protestant/Catholic
  - Liberal/conservative
  - Labor/management
  - Rural/urban
  - Union/nonunion

These examples will lead you to think of others in your own community. Whatever the splits that exist, *a separate power structure develops for each segment.*

- **Power Group.** Most times, there is a pool of 10 to 25 persons who comprise the power in the community. Within this group, there may be some specialization or structuring by topic area. For example, only three or four of this group act together on any given issue, that is, a new facility for the free clinic. At the same time, four or five may combine to help the local school build a scholarship fund or assist in a rezoning issue. It is entirely likely that one or more serve on the boards of the organizations that various members of the group feel compelled to help.

From experience, there will be less specialization by topic as the community size decreases, so it is quite possible that in a town of 1,500 to 5,000, most of the key leaders will be involved in all significant community issues. That said, the *power group* is the more usual type of power structure found and has a number of implications for development officers wishing to instigate some change: a) the principal leaders need to be identified for each topic; b) there are communications networks within the pool; and c) power groups change membership from time to time, so it is important to identify and assess key leaders with some regularity.

Now that you have the concept in mind, you can begin the process of defining the potential power groups in your area. These may fall into the following categories:

- Geographical
  - Service area
  - Municipality
  - Neighborhoods or subdivisions
- Organizational
  - Alumni/ae
  - Civic club
  - Fraternal
  - Trade associations/unions
  - Professional
  - Political
  - Religious
  - Chamber of Commerce
  - Business development

Identify about four topic areas to which you may link power players to your organization (art, medicine, youth, education, urban renewal, etc.) Try to keep the topics somewhat broad, unless your organization's appeal is extremely narrow.

The next step is to recruit board members and other willing volunteers both to select those to be interviewed and to make the calls. Get enough volunteers involved so that no one has more than three interviews to conduct. Sometimes is it best to use a team approach with one volunteer making the presentation and the other conducting the interview. Training for this ad hoc committee is also relatively simple, consisting of preparing them to make the presentation with PowerPoint, and making certain that they understand the importance of asking each question in the order listed to get the best results.

The number of individuals to be identified and interviewed depends upon the size of the community or segment of a larger metropolitan region. We will call these people "knowers" because they are selected on the basis of their occupations. They are in positions most likely to hear, see, and learn about issues and people in your service area and community. The following chart will give you guidance in selecting the number needed to have the best results.

Size of Community	Number of Knowers to be Interviewed
250—1,000	5
1,001—2,500	7
2,501—5,000	8
5,001—10,000	10
10,001—100,000	15
100,001—500,000	25

In the computer world, we often hear the statement "garbage in . . . garbage out." We can keep that in mind when making the selection of key people to be interviewed. The individuals who are selected should come from a cross-section of your community (bankers, editors, business owners/managers, etc.) who are well-positioned truly to know who the power players are who might be interested in hearing about your organization. When leading the meeting to identify those who will be contacted, start with the people with whom your volunteers interact and do business, and work outward from there. Once a few names are on the flip chart, others will come to mind, and the list of names will grow. At that point, you can prioritize and make assignments.

It is a good idea to schedule meeting "check points" throughout the process, usually every three weeks. Not only does this keep everyone on track, but additional names will emerge from the interviews that you may want to add to your call list. At the conclusion of the interview period, the meeting will focus on identifying the "power players" who have surfaced. Retain all those persons named two to three or more times. The top key leaders in all issue areas constitute the power group for your community.

Conducting the Interview with the Knower   Previously, we suggested that a team of volunteers can be an effective way of making appointments and conducting interviews. However, whether one or two volunteers are on the call, begin the meeting by making a brief presentation about your organization—mission, history, service, goals, financial needs, and so on—and by answering any questions that may arise from the case statement.

After the presentation, ask the knower if he or she would be willing to answer a few questions that would be helpful to the organization's development. Give assurance that the information will not be attributed to him or her, that the conversation is confidential, and that only what is learned will be used to assist in developmental planning.

Typical questions that may be asked are:

- Does the case statement provide sufficient information about the organization to help understand its mission, purpose, goals, and financial needs in a clear, concise way?

- Are there questions that yet should be answered?

- Now that you know more about this organization, are you or your company more likely to support it?

- Who are the persons of influence and/or wealth in our community you know? Which of them do you think would be interested in knowing more about our organization? (If asked how many, it is best to limit the number to 10.) In what other organizations are these individuals interested or involved?

- Which of these persons would be most interested in (state topic area)? How do you rate yourself as a community leader?

When the interviews are completed, summarize the results making note of the number of times each leader—power player—is named. As a general rule, if five to eight individuals were interviewed, retain those names mentioned two or more times. If more than eight were interviewed, keep those named three or more times.

If the knowers were selected with care, you will have identified the members of the power structure to whom you need to tell the story of your organization. And remember, it is very important to understand that this exercise of identifying and cultivating the interest and involvement of your community's power players is essential for the long-term health of your organization.

Social power exists in every community, with key leaders relating to each other and acting in concert with each other on many community issues. Most legitimate power is based on influence, not command, and these leaders are normally aware of their influence. They also know that they keep their influential positions through their support or opposition to public and private projects. The challenge for a nonprofit is to capture the attention and involvement of enough power players to help make possible the achievement of your mission of service.

Managing Your Major Gift Prospects

In the history of donor relationship building, there are two people who have effectively helped to focus the efforts of the development process—Philip Kotler, who was discussed earlier, and Buck Smith. Mr. Smith introduced a system called "MOVES"—major-gifts management that provides a clear set of guidelines to establish and enhance a relationship with each potential donor. The MOVES method helps the individual development officer and the volunteer/staff cultivation team to use their time and energy in the highest and wisest way.

MOVES is a system that enables the small and large development shops to manage a major gifts program, measure its progress step by step, and raise major dollars on a continuing, consistent basis.

A MOVE is defined as a planned action with a major prospect that is *unanticipated* by the prospect and is designed to *move* the individual to an improved understanding, acceptance, and appreciation of your organization.

Use these steps to begin your MOVES program:

- List as many prospective major donors as you can.
- From what you currently know, place each of them in one of three categories of potential —Highest, Middle Range, and Lowest.
- Choose the prospects with whom you will work first. The MOVES process forces you to make choices, to prioritize your time and resources and that of your volunteers.
- Assign yourself, other staff members, and volunteers to each prospect. If you are a one-person shop (and are also the executive director), be prudent about the number of prospects you have on your list. Remember, too, this can give you a good strategy to involve key board members to help.
- Plan the first Move for each priority prospect. In most cases, this will be a cultivation Move and may involve a breakfast or lunch meeting, office visit, dinner party, and the like to introduce the prospect to the organization or bring new information to the prospect. Implement the Move, evaluate, and plan the next step(s).

Though we have specified individuals in the above, the process works equally well for corporations and foundations. After all, the task is to engage individuals in your mission and services. The ultimate goal is to MOVE the potential donor to the point where the individual understands how his/her need is being met by giving money to meet a need your organization has identified. As we have noted previously, this is known in marketing terms as an "exchange relationship" where both parties get something they want and need. Therefore, as you identify major prospects, do what research you can, plan cultivation MOVES, and, ultimately, ask for a gift, remember that you must describe your organization and its financial needs in terms of how it meets the individual prospect's needs.

Obtaining Support from Corporations and Foundations

Many board members and volunteers of nonprofits make an assumption that the fundraising program should focus on obtaining grants from foundations and corporations. While these entities should absolutely be a part of your marketing and fundraising strategies, it is important to remind your volunteer leadership that the majority of contributions are made by individuals. *Giving USA* reports that of the $307.65 billion given in 2008 (the most recent year results are known at the time of this writing), individual Americans gave 82 percent of the total while foundations (13%) and corporations (5%) made up the rest. Your priority, therefore, should always be the identification, qualification, cultivation, and solicitation of individuals whether you are planning an annual fund, major gift, or capital campaign effort. With that point made, you certainly want to spend an appropriate amount of your time in raising money from corporations and foundations that your research has shown may give money in support of your organization.

When it comes to working with corporations and foundations, however, there can be a tendency to think of entities rather than people. We forget that regardless of foundation center summaries, application procedures, required documentation, and all the rest, you are still interacting with the people who run them. There will always be a "gatekeeper" through whom you must gain passage for your funding need, followed by others who serve on committees and boards. These individuals represent cultivation opportunities—individuals with whom you should work to help them better understand, accept, and appreciate your nonprofit. The greater ownership these corporate and foundation people feel, the greater the chance that your proposal will receive serious consideration and funding.

Careful research is required to learn which corporations and foundations may be interested in your organization and/or one or more of the services you offer to your patients/clients/students. A subscription to the online *Foundation Directory* is a worthwhile expenditure because it gives you immediate returns on narrowing the potential grant-making sources for you to approach. If you are not able to subscribe, your local library should have the latest edition of the *Foundation Directory*. Another good source of information is the individual 990 tax filings that should be found on the websites of these grant makers.

Once you have developed your list of likely corporate and foundation suspects, determine which of your organizational projects/needs in which each might be interested, based on their history of giving. Write an abbreviated letter describing your organization and the project to send to each potential funding source, asking if there is interest in their receiving a full proposal. If not already known, ask for an application, proposal requirements, and deadlines. You may also request a meeting or telephone conference; however, such are often difficult to arrange.

Following the paring of the list to your best prospects, draft the proposal and accumulate the data that each corporation and foundation requires. Send each exactly what is specified—and no more, in spite of the urge to include additional information. This shows that you can follow direction and, more importantly, that you are showing respect for their guidelines and processes.

Even having been intelligent in your research, identifying the best prospects and doing everything you have been asked by the funders to do, you may still not receive the grant you have requested. Use this as a way to receive counseling from the "gatekeeper" to help you do a better job in the future. Continue to build a good relationship with this person, and you will improve your chances for a positive result the next time you submit.

A final point—if you have the budget, it is advisable to use an experienced grant writer to research and prepare your proposal. There are highly qualified people who have spent their careers in the field who will save you mountains of time and deliver a product that will give you the best chance of success.

PLANNED GIVING—ANOTHER WAY TO RAISE MAJOR GIFTS

We know we should do it. We have been to professional meetings and heard of the success of others who have done it. We even belong to our local planned giving council and attend the lunch meetings. But, we just have not brought ourselves to the point of action in beginning a planned giving program. After all, we rationalize:

- We need contributions to balance the operating budget, pay for new facilities, and equipment now. We are concerned what would happen if our donors focused on future giving.
- We don't have time and/or staff to deal with a planned giving program.
- We don't have the necessary expertise.

- We don't have enough budget to buy the materials, get the training, and so on.

All of these excuses have degrees of validity, especially in development offices that have one professional and, if lucky, some secretarial staff support. The pressures to produce gift income in the current fiscal year are real. These dollars mean programs are funded and staff members get paid on time.

Perhaps, the greatest truest reason that planned giving is put in the development closet, however, is *FEAR*. If we would eavesdrop on the thoughts of many development officers, we would probably hear:

> "People spend their entire careers as planned giving professionals and are constantly studying to keep up with changes in the law, new plans to recommend—I could never learn this stuff in a hundred lifetimes. Unless we hire a specialist, I do not feel comfortable or adequate in tackling this."

If you do not currently have an active planned giving program, you are denying your organization a rich source of future dollars that can be the difference between financial stability and budgetary stress. These next pages will be devoted to giving you a practical path to planned giving success, as well as increasing your level of comfort.

The Definition of Planned Giving

The place to begin, as the old expression goes, is at the beginning. Let us first agree on what we mean about planned giving.

> *Planned giving describes a gift that is committed during the donor's lifetime with the benefits of the gift becoming available to your organization at a future date.*

Planned giving uses tax, financial, and estate-planning techniques to make it possible for the donor to provide a substantial gift to your organization, while enabling the maximum tax and financial benefits for the donor and, in most cases, the donor's family.

Using planned-giving techniques has often made it possible for a donor to make a larger contribution than would have been possible during his or her lifetime. In addition, careful planning may dramatically reduce the cost of making the gift.

Principles for Your Planned-Giving Program

There are seven principles that should guide a planned-giving program:

1. Focus on telling the story of your organization, not just the tax savings features of one or more planned giving vehicles. We have written it before and write it again—people do not usually make contributions because of the tax deductions. They support causes to which they feel connected—that touch them in ways that meet special needs in their lives. Current tax law does inform them of the size, the kind, and the timing of their gifts, just as it does in all such decisions.

2. Show how giving to your organization can be the means to enable prospects to accomplish something important to them that they could not do otherwise.

3. Build the list of prospects from those who know your organization best—trustees, key volunteers, alumni, parents, grateful patients, etc. For planned giving, prospects should be 60 years of age and older.

4. Use those who have made their own estate-related commitment to promote your planned-giving program.

5. Get those who regularly counsel people about estate and tax matters involved.

6. Remember that a planned gift is just another way to make a major gift.

7. Planned gifts happen when someone (like you) makes them happen.

1, 2, 3, 4—Steps to Creating and Operating Your Planned-Giving Program

Here are the four steps for you to follow in beginning your foray into planned giving.

Step 1. Know What You Don't Know

If you have not entered the world of planned giving until now, you may feel inadequate to the task ahead. You may suffer from a "mental lockup" just thinking about the subject. To you, the term "crummy trust" is a pretty good way to describe the whole business. That, for you, is the *bad news* about planned giving.

The *good news* is: You don't have to be an expert in order to promote planned giving for your organization, nor should you be. Let the experts be expert and use their help and advice. It is unwise for any development officer to talk with prospects about anything he or she is not qualified to discuss.

You know about your organization and its needs. Talk about that and learn how your prospect's needs can be met though supporting one or more of your organization's priorities. A good development officer can stimulate a donor to think about options, provide information, help prospects see the vision of what their giving can mean, and create opportunities for donor recognition.

In the course of your work, you will become more familiar with terms and types of planned-giving vehicles. But—recognize your limitations. Professional help should always be recommended to the prospect when there is an interest in making any deferred gift. As the poet Alexander Pope wrote:

> A little learning is a dangerous thing
> Drink deep, or taste not the Pierian Spring;
> There shallow draughts intoxicate the brain,
> And drinking largely sobers us again.

Step 2. Recruit a Planned-Giving Support Team

Once you understand that promoting planned giving does not require you to be an expert on the subject, the next step is to identify and recruit some professional help. To be sure, there is more than one approach to creating a Planned Giving Advisory Committee. We recommend that you recruit a committee of those who are experts in the many facets of planned giving, including CPAs, tax attorneys, bank trust officers, CLUs, and other financial planners. Their job is not to identify and solicit planned gifts—that would be problematic ethically for any of them. Their task is to be the solid professional foundation for your program.

In addition to providing information and advice, they should:

- Recommend to the board the policies and guidelines for your organization's planned giving program.
- Plan and conduct seminars on estate planning and planned-giving segments of your constituency.
- Write articles on planned giving for your newsletter or magazine.
- Serve as a resource to the board and to the major gifts committee.
- Serve as advisors to prospects who request information and do not have professional advisors.
- Review and approve brochures used in promoting planned giving.

Step 3. Establish Policies and Guideline

A written and approved statement of policies and guidelines for the planned giving program is essential. Such policies and guidelines should come from the planned giving advisory committee and will usually address:

- Who will cultivate and accept planned gifts?
- What types of planned gifts will be promoted and accepted—Bequests? Charitable trusts? Gift annuities? Charitable lead trusts? Life insurance?

- What gifts of real property will be accepted and under what conditions?
- What gifts of tangible personal property will be accepted?
- How will gifts of listed or unlisted securities be accepted and handled?
- What will be the limitations and procedures for restricted gifts?
- What is the function and authority of the Planned Giving Advisory Committee?

Additional procedures may be necessary if your organization is to act as trustee, issue annuity contracts, and the like. Remember, though, that too many rules concerning procedures can be worse than no rules at all. Ask for copies of similar statements from other organizations in your area. If you have the services of a consultant, he or she will be able to provide a basic copy that the professionals on your committee can use as a guide.

Step 4. Get Started with a Wills Bequest Program

No matter how small your development program and staff, it is possible to begin encouraging prospects and donors to think of your organization when making their wills. Using direct mail as the primary means to contact your prospects, a wills bequest program can be conducted to: 1) Identify friends (alumni, etc.) of your organization in whose wills you are already included; 2) Invite appropriate constituents (age 50+) to consider putting your organization in their wills; and 3) Provide a means to recognize during their lifetimes estate-related commitments to your organization.

Following this chapter is a template for setting up a wills bequest program. By starting with the most basic of planned giving techniques, you will give yourself the space and time to increase in knowledge and confidence as your program grows. You will also raise more money for your organization both now and in future resources.

CAPITAL CAMPAIGNS

When the big bands were the rage, Tommy Dorsey had one of the best. Among his hits was a number titled "The Dipsy Doodle." The lyrics began:

> The dipsy doodle is the thing to beware
> The dipsy doodle will get in your hair
> And if it gets you, it couldn't be worse
> The things you say will come out in reverse. . . .

Without pretending the words get better from this point, the tune comes to mind when reviewing, analyzing, and preparing to assist organizations who have capital campaigns that have stalled or are having difficulty gaining traction with their major constituency.

The method used to prepare for a capital effort is the best predictor of success or stagnation. It is unfortunate that campaign planning activities that should come first come too much later, if at all. The "dipsy doodle" planning leads to ineffective implementation and frustration on the parts of the CEO, staff members, and most important, volunteers. In the following paragraphs, we will discuss the campaign planning pitfalls to avoid and make some suggestions on positive action steps to prepare for a successful campaign.

At Last—The Truth about Capital Campaigns Revealed!

The very thought of having to launch and manage a capital campaign often has the same effect on development officers as sunlight on the legendary Count Dracula. Certainly, there are particular pressures on the CEO and the development staff during a campaign. However, the major funding goals that are addressed by the capital effort—if they truly are required to meet the organization's needs—are the same ones that would have to be met in any case. Organizational needs do not go away, but they must be met for the nonprofit's current and future health in meeting its mission of service. A capital campaign, then, is the *strategic means* that your organization uses to achieve its major funding requirements.

The capital campaign should be viewed as an enhancement to your overall development program, not an addition to it. The campaign method is chosen because it gives your organization at least six opportunities for growth and visibility:

1. To raise major gifts for facilities and endowment
2. To build new or renewed enthusiasm for your mission and program
3. To train new leadership
4. To raise giving sights of your constituents
5. To broaden your base of supporters
6. To provide greater publicity for your organization and higher visibility for your ongoing funding needs

It is also important to consider the capital campaign as a comprehensive effort that will enable your nonprofit to improve its ability to raise funds—annual and capital—well beyond the campaign's completion. Some organizations include the annual funding needs within the campaign itself. In this way, you are assured both that the annual needs are emphasized and that everyone in your constituency can be a part of meeting your organization's total funding goals. However, even if you do not choose to make the annual fund a formal part of the campaign, it should be vigorously conducted with goals of increasing donors and amounts of gifts.

Components of a Capital Campaign

There are four components of a capital campaign:

1. **The Case for Support**—Why is the money needed and why should anyone care?

   The process your organization uses to determine campaign goals will have an impact on the potential for your success. As we covered in an earlier chapter, it is highly advisable to include those key persons who have the ability to make and influence major gifts in planning and finalizing the campaign goals. It is much easier to build excitement and commitment at the start than to engage people later on, no matter how attractive the campaign brochure. There is an old but true saying that applies here: "If you want advice, ask for money. If you want money, ask for advice."

2. **The Pool of Major Gifts Prospects**—Who will give the money?

   Year after year, the American Association of Fundraising Counsel's report shows that around 90% of all contributions in the United States come from individuals, either during lifetime or through estates. Therefore, your pool of available major prospects should be rated and related to the campaign gift chart to determine if, indeed, you have sufficient depth to plan and launch a campaign. The Perotti Principle also applies—80 percent of the campaign goal will be given by 20 percent of your donors. In addition, the ratio of prospects to actual donors is about 3 or 4 to 1.

3. **The Campaign Leadership**—Who will ask for the money?

   A well-motivated and trained development officer is an asset to the successful implementation of a campaign. Equally important is having a CEO who will commit the time and energy necessary to help motivate volunteers and actively participate in raising major gifts. In addition, members of the board should be committed to achieving the goals of the campaign by making the best capital gift each can and serve in appropriate campaign leadership roles.

4. **The Campaign Plan**—How will the money be raised?

   A successful campaign follows a well-thought-out action plan that includes:
   - A statement of campaign objectives and other benefits that may be derived from its conduct
   - The time line of the campaign
   - A chart of the number and sizes of gifts required to meet the goal
   - Job descriptions of the campaign chair(s), steering committee, and other committees

- Policies regarding naming facilities and endowed funds
- Policies for the kind of gifts that will be accepted
- Specific information on campaign reporting, promotion, and publicity
- A statement concerning when the campaign will enter the public phase

To Study or Not to Study—A Critical Question

It is fair to say that the first words heard when a capital campaign is contemplated are: "We need a feasibility study to see if we can raise that kind of money!"

Do you need a feasibility study? The answer for most organizations is—maybe. Before you decide, ask these questions:

- What will you learn by conducting a study that you do not already know?

- How will conducting a study improve your ability to raise major gifts?

The challenge in raising capital support is moving major prospects into a closer relationship with your organization, building understanding and appreciation of its needs (ownership), and showing how support of one or more campaign objectives *will meet the prospects' needs to make a gift commensurate with their individual potentials.*

Experience has shown that the best approach to engaging board members, major prospects, and other key persons who are essential for success is to invite them to participate in planning the capital campaign. To review, properly conceived and conducted, the planning activity will:

- Enable the CEO to share his/her vision for the future

- Bring a fresh perspective to the proposed projects

- Uncover and deal with perceptions that may hinder your ability to raise major dollars

- Cultivate board members and other major prospects who will needed for the campaign to succeed

- Develop committed campaign volunteer leadership

- Develop new candidates for board membership

Following the campaign planning, board, senior staff, and campaign leadership can schedule small group sessions and/or one-on-one interviews with major prospects to advise them of the organization's plans, how they were derived, assess interest, and get feedback. In this way, the organization's leadership can learn the same information from a prospect/donor that would be revealed in a study—with the added benefit of having the opportunity for strengthening the relationship that can lead to the prospect's involvement and major giving.

If the decision is made that a campaign readiness study would be the appropriate first step, the consultant should:

- Examine all aspects of the development program to make certain that the organization is prepared to conduct a campaign (development audit).

- Interview key prospects to assess ownership and willingness to support financially the campaign objectives.

- Provide a campaign plan and time line if the assessment shows the organization is ready to proceed.

- If not ready for the tested campaign goals, provide recommendations that would enable the organization in the shortest period of time to be able to conduct the campaign.

The study should not be used to discourage you. It is merely a snapshot of your current situation. The study should, in fact, provide the keys to what must be done to enable the accomplishment of your capital goals. Remember—the capital campaign is a means to meet identified financial needs and is only a success when it accomplishes those funding objectives.

Capital Campaign Planning Pitfalls

Here is a listing of the most common reasons that capital campaign get off on the wrong foot:

- Only the CEO has the "vision" of the organization's future—and does not permit any tinkering by board members and other important organizational players.

- Those who must make major gifts for the campaign to succeed have not been a part of the goal setting and have no ownership of them.

- The organization has not had an ongoing program to identify, cultivate, and solicit major gifts.

- There has not been a consistent effort to communicate the organization's needs through the annual fund and other publications.

- The campaign was announced before 60% or more of the goal had been reached.

- The board is weak.

- Volunteers have not been regularly used by the organization.

- The campaign is viewed as a separate activity from the total development program.

- Identification and rating of the available pool of prospects has not been realistically done.

Organize to Win

Several years ago, a client organization was preparing to recruit the volunteer who would chair the capital campaign and be members of the campaign steering committee. The organization's president was strongly advised to ask for a leadership gift, along with the request for the individual to chair the campaign. It was clear that the president was not comfortable with this, and suggested that it was unnecessary to do so since the person would know that a capital gift would be expected. The main concern was securing a prominent campaign chair.

The call was made and the individual responded positively to chairing the campaign. However, he was not solicited for a gift because the president was too uncomfortable about asking for money and, at the same time, elated that the campaign chair was secured. He would, the president assured us, make his commitment in due course. The campaign chair provided leadership in securing other members of the steering committee, asking them and others for capital gifts. However, he never made a gift to the campaign, and, as a result, opportunities for several major gifts were lost.

Many of us in the profession can relate to this experience. It is far too common for presidents and board members to be reluctant to solicit the appropriate gift from one who is being asked to serve in a leadership role for the campaign. Yet, failing to do so places the organization, the campaign, and the volunteer in untenable positions. The story emphasizes a truth that all of us know even when we do not follow it. It is this: *A volunteer should not ask anyone to do anything the volunteer has not done. To do otherwise robs the volunteer of the most effective tool he or she has—credibility—and will make the achievement of campaign goals less likely.*

Therefore, once the list of potential campaign volunteers has been prepared (and each candidate has been properly researched), consider these steps to building your campaign leadership:

- Qualify the candidates according to the position you wish them to hold within the campaign structure.
- Determine the gift that each will be asked to consider, including any naming opportunity that would be appropriate to their ability and interest.
- Determine who should accompany the CEO in making the call on each candidate.
- Agree on who should make the appointment and several dates that fit both persons' schedules.

- Plan, with the involvement of the chief development officer, the roles the CEO, board member, or other volunteer will play in the meeting (who will discuss the campaign, who will ask for the commitment, etc.).

- Arm the solicitors with all of the information needed fully to inform the candidate about the campaign and his/her role in it.

- Provide appropriate information (a written proposal, drawings, etc.) to support the request for the candidate's financial commitment.

- Be absolutely honest and frank about what the candidate is being asked to do and the staff support that he or she can expect.

Asking for money at the same time that one requests the prospect to accept a significant volunteer responsibility can be daunting to many otherwise strong CEOs and board members. Yet, it must be done if the campaign is to begin on a firm foundation. It is never wise to ask a person to serve as a campaign leader and assume that the gift commitment will come as a matter of course. Experience has shown that even if the pledge is ultimately made, it is not usually in the range that gives the volunteer credibility with the remainder of your supportive constituency.

Selecting Campaign Leadership   Great care should be taken in screening those whom you will be asking to serve as volunteer leaders for the capital effort. Normally, the list of candidates will be put together by a committee composed of the CEO, chair of the board, chair of the development committee of the board, and the chief development officer.

As candidates are being considered, ask these questions to help give you and your nonprofit leadership guidance in making the best choices:

- Does the candidate have a history of supportive interest in your organization?

- Does the candidate have a positive image among those of your constituencies who are familiar with him/her?

- Does the candidate have knowledge of and influence with those who must become major donors to the campaign?

- Can the candidate expand the knowledge and influence of your organization into groups not previously supportive?

- Can the candidate make a gift commensurate with the level of contributions for which he or she will be asking?

- Is the candidate ready to be asked to serve in the leadership position for which he or she is being considered?

Campaign Organization The size and number of committees needed to operate a successful campaign are dependent upon the type of organization and the goals of the capital effort. In some organizations, the campaign steering committee serves as the body that both directs the campaign and solicits leadership and major gifts. In other organizations, specialized subcommittees of the campaign steering committee are set up for particular purposes and constituencies. Here are descriptions of the committees most commonly employed:

- **Campaign Steering Committee**—is responsible for providing overall guidance for the campaign. Its membership includes the campaign chair (s), the CEO, the chief development officer, the board development chair, and the chairs of the other campaign sub-committees. The steering committee:
  - reviews and approves campaign plans and materials
  - identifies and recruits other campaign volunteers
  - identifies, cultivates, and solicits leadership and major gifts prospects
  - provides guidance and motivation to campaign volunteers
  - helps keep the focus on seeking major gifts from individuals
- **Trustee/Director Leadership Gifts Committee**—is led by the chair of the board. Committee members are asked for their gifts and then assist in soliciting financial leadership commitments from other trustees.
- **Rating Committee**—is composed of the steering committee members and selected other knowledgeable individuals to review the available major suspects and assess their potential, according to the campaign gift chart.
- **Major Gifts Committee**—in concert with members of the steering committee, has as its primary responsibility the identification, cultivation, and solicitation of major support from individuals. In some capital campaigns, the steering committee assumes this function.
- **Corporations and Foundations Committee**—works with the development staff members in identifying business and foundation prospects and assisting in building support from them.
- **Annual Fund Committee**—in comprehensive campaigns, keeps the focus on annual giving, and helps identify prospects for the major gifts committee.
- **Marketing and Events Committee**—is useful in the creation of campaign materials, planning and executing small group gatherings, and the announcement of the public phase of the campaign.

Your campaign plan and how your volunteers are best organized depend upon a variety of factors. The most important factor is to have a written plan of action with responsibilities clearly defined and a time line for campaign objectives.

THE ROLE OF SPECIAL EVENTS IN DEVELOPMENT

Those of us old enough to remember or are fans of classic movies will be familiar with the Mickey Rooney/Judy Garland films. In the ones that I recall, there was a pressing and immediate need for funds, no one in the group had any, and if money were not raised quickly, the theater, project, and so on, would be shut down.

Invariably, Mickey or Judy would propose putting on a benefit show. This was done in record time with a surplus of excellent talent and music, and more patrons at the event than could be accommodated comfortably. Of course, the funds were raised, the theatre/project was saved, the curtain music swelled, and all was well with the world.

Unfortunately, the Hollywood movie formula for raising funds is too often the venue of choice for real-world nonprofits to the detriment of building productive, long-term development programs.

The most extreme example of this reliance on special events to raise money occurred several years ago at an organization we were privileged to serve as counsel. While other event-type fundraisers were conducted during the year, most of the development and public relations staff time was dedicated to staging a major event during the holidays. Business sponsorships were sought, marketing materials were created, and contracts were negotiated and signed—activities that consumed several months. The event was always a great success in that it was well done, attracted many people, and provided a good public image for the organization. However, it did fail on one important count. This major event that distracted development staff from building donor relationships and raising annual and major gifts never made any money.

Granted, this is an extreme example, but to one extent or another, event fundraising does require a great deal of staff and volunteer effort. Therefore, do not undertake any event without determining its worth on levels beyond raising money.

What Do You Want to Accomplish?

There are a number of good reasons for your organization to use special events:

- To celebrate your organization, its mission, and its programs
- To recognize special people—generous donors, outstanding staff/faculty, and prominent individuals in the field of your organization's specialty

- To motivate volunteers and donors
- To introduce new people to your organization
- To raise funds

You may add other reasons to the list, but you will note that raising money is the last consideration. Other compelling factors should outweigh fundraising by a considerable degree before your organization agrees to, plans, and executes a special event.

The Developmental Special Event

The very best special event is one that enables leadership, supporters, and new prospects to come together in an atmosphere that promotes greater understanding, acceptance, and appreciation of your organization's mission and purpose. Properly conceived and conducted, your organization should be in a better position to raise funds after the event than before or during. The event should lead to an expanded list of potential major donors and open avenues of approaches that did not previously exist.

A developmental special event can take many forms:

- A formal or informal dinner that may include a dance and/or a silent auction
- A reception/lunch/dinner for a selected list of prospects hosted by a board member or a key volunteer
- A play or musical event for selected donors and prospects with a reception following
- A holiday party or open house hosted by the CEO or a board member

One of the most useful developmental events is the annual dinner for donors and prospective donors and is known by many names (Founders Day Dinner, President's Dinner, Celebration Banquet, etc.). A main attribute of this kind of affair is that you have control over the setting, the participants, and the messages. In planning the event, make certain that the program includes:

- Information on the organization's achievements during the past year
- Recognition of those who have served your organization in special ways— as volunteers or major donors
- Expression of the vision of what your organization is becoming or can become through the involvement and support of the attendees
- As appropriate, involvement of those who are benefiting from your non-profit's program (e.g., student giving invocation, client expressing how life has changed, etc.)

There are other kinds of events that can have an appropriate place in your annual program. These are the familiar golf tournament, walkathon, auction, festival featuring food and carnival activities, and the like. Remember that, in general, the cost in staff time will always be high without a commensurate return in funds. Here are some thoughts on operating such events to receive the maximum benefit:

- Get a business to sponsor and take complete responsibility for the event. Your involvement would be to attend and pick up a check.
- Use a committee of volunteers whose members enjoy planning and running a special event.
- Actively think about the ways to disseminate information about your organization during the event.
- Consider hiring a professional event manager. In many cases, this is the most cost-efficient way to conduct a successful special event.

Finally, have a plan for following up with each person who participated in the event to let them know how their round of golf, bid on an auction item, made a difference in the lives of those you serve. This is an important first step toward building productive, supportive relationships with those who, before the event, may only have had a nodding acquaintance of your organization. Whatever the event, the most significant aspect is the systematic follow-up with everyone who participated.

KEEPING THE FRIENDS YOU HAVE MADE

It is fitting that we complete this chapter with a reminder that practicing effective development means you must be fully engaged in marketing activities, not sales. Your role as a development professional is to build long-term relationships with each member of your constituency. Therefore, your daily planning and working to enable multiple satisfactory exchanges with your organization must be a priority, so that members of your target audiences feel increasingly greater satisfaction and enjoyment in being associated with your nonprofit as volunteers and as donors.

Keeping the donor's interest is, for the most part, an individualized activity. There are techniques, of course, that will work for most everyone; however, you cannot design a "one size fits all" approach and expect to be successful. Just as cultivation and solicitation of the gift was prepared and executed for each prospect, so must the program to retain and continue to build the relationship with the donor.

Much of what succeeds in development has roots in the Golden Rule. Think seriously about how you would react to a contemplated action directed toward a prospect. When you do, you will come to a better understanding of both the individual prospect and yourself.

There are two basic approaches to keeping a donor's interest in your nonprofit. The differences occur in the tools available to you and the expectations of each donor.

1. *Saying Thank You.* While this is the most fundamental expression, there are multiple ways to express appreciation.
    a. Send a letter of thanks with the appropriate tax information from the CEO or the chief development officer, depending on the size of your nonprofit and the amount of the gift. Usually, any amount over $500 (and any gift from a board member) gets the CEO's signature. In some cases, a personal PS is a good touch to make personal the standard response letter. We NEVER advise sending an impersonal thank-you card, no matter how small the gift. Your response should reflect your honest appreciation for whatever it received.
    b. A personal note from the volunteer solicitor is an especially good idea for special annual and capital gifts. These are best when they are handwritten.
    c. When the gift benefits a client or student, you should consider asking the beneficiary to write a note of thanks to the donor. Always exercise control over the content of the note, however, by making suggestions and by reading each one before they are sealed and mailed.

2. *Showing more tangible appreciation.* There are a number of ways, most cost effective, to give donors appropriate public recognition. These methods also serve to motivate others to begin to give or to become more generous in their giving.
    a. Listing in the Honor Roll of Donors in the Annual Report is a time-honored method of recognizing donors. There are a number of categories within the listing that can be effectively used if you have recognition clubs.
    b. At significant levels of giving, donors can be recognized on wall plaques at your organization's offices. For annual giving, it is important to update the plaque on an annual basis to reflect only those who qualify for the particular fiscal year. When donors know their names will be removed unless they continue to give, most are highly motivated to keep current.

c. A variation of the annual recognition using an updatable plaque is to present the significant donor with one that can be displayed in his/her office or home. The plaque should have a minimum of five to a maximum of ten years worth of spaces for date tabs to be inserted. You may be amazed at how important filling in those blanks becomes to the donor.

d. Lapel pins, certificates, and wallet cards are important for some recognition groups, especially ones that recognize those who have made estate-related commitments to your organization.

e. There are some interesting and creative ways to show tangible recognition that may touch a donor more than any plaque. Consider whether you have a picture of a project or a campus building that can be framed and presented to the donor. Is there a picture that shows the work of your nonprofit in action (building a home, delivering food, etc.) that could be given to the donor whose gifts made the work possible? A particularly moving token of appreciation can be something as simple as a piece of letterhead with the signatures and notes of the clients or students who have been beneficiaries of the donor's gifts. Placed in Plexiglas, this document, which can be displayed on a table or wall, can be more meaningful and powerful than any other expression of thanks.

Perhaps, at the simplest level, you must remember to remind donors continually why they gave to your organization in the first place. This means being "hands on" with your special donors beyond the newsletters and annual report. You can do this through personal notes keeping them updated on the project they helped fund, having a reception with beneficiaries of their giving, and visiting with them to bring them news and discuss current/future successes and needs. In addition, you can remember birthdays, anniversaries, and other special occasions important to them. You can invite them to special events and educational seminars. Sometimes, just making a phone call at regular intervals can mean a great deal, most especially with elderly donors.

With younger donors, Facebook, Twitter, and other social media give you opportunities to stay in touch. Tempting as it may be, however, to send a "Tweet" every day, most people will appreciate receiving information that is really interesting and important and not be deluged by your organization.

Last, when it is appropriate, invite significant donors to serve as volunteers. Keeping them involved in "hands-on" service is the very best way to cement a long-term relationship. Both younger and older donors will appreciate being asked to help with those activities that are within their abilities.

In Summary

Much has been covered in this chapter in programs and techniques to raise the dollars your organization requires to meet its mission. Let us conclude with these reminders:

- Staff and volunteers can fall into the special events trap, believing this is an easy way to raise money without actually having to ask for it. Ultimately, they find that this is the most unproductive, time-consuming activity in which they could be engaged. However, special events do have a strategic developmental role to play in your complete development program.

- Avoid practicing over-cultivation with the same group of donors because you do not want to face the possibility of rejection by reaching out to new people. Expand your comfort zone and lead others to broaden their circle of potential donors.

- Always create a plan of action with measureable objectives and a time line for each task. Using a "seat-of-the-pants" approach will not produce the results you need, and you will never really know if you're just busy or actually doing something valuable for your nonprofit.

The beginning of embarking on a productive path for your development program is to impose the discipline of creating—on paper—a development plan of action that incorporates all of the objectives that must be accomplished within the fiscal year—both marketing and fundraising. Next, make a list of those prospects who will expand your call list, set a weekly goal for face-to-face contacts, and begin the work of making new and renewed friends for your organizations. The MOVES prospect management program offers an excellent approach to identifying, planning, and working with major prospects.

ANNUAL FUND COMMITTEE JOB DESCRIPTION

Overview

The Annual Fund Committee will review, coordinate, develop plans and procedures, and recommend policies for the annual giving program of (Name of Organization). The committee shall work to raise funds for annual operating needs and special programs identified by the organization, and to develop a wide base of contributors who support the organization on a regular, annual basis.

Objectives

1. To assist in the creation of an annual giving emphasis to each constituent group in order to acquire new donors, retain current donors, and encourage donors to move to higher levels of annual giving.

2. To counsel on the core messages in annual giving appeals.

3. To review and provide advice on brochures and other materials used in annual giving.

4. To recommend methods for acknowledging and recognizing annual gifts, including benefits for each annual giving club.

5. To organize and conduct a program of personal contact of selected prospects for annual gifts.

6. To identify prospective major donors and forward them to the major gifts committee.

7. To review materials used in the encouragement of gifts to honor and memorialize individuals.

8. To help identify and recruit other volunteers in obtaining annual support.

9. To help the CEO and staff in the cultivating and soliciting selected top major annual prospects.

Committee Membership

The committee will be composed of representatives of each constituent group to be solicited through the Annual Giving Program. The CEO of the organization shall appoint the chair of the committee.

AF SOLICITATION LETTERS

Kickoff Letter

(DATE)

Ima Donor
555 Homey Lane
Your City, State ZIP

Dear Ima:

Thank you for your support of (Name of Organization) last year. Your gift of $_____ enabled the organization to reach a number of young parents in our community who were struggling with their children and their emotions. Through the (Name) program, (Name of Organization) provided the knowledge and skills necessary for them to deal in positive ways with their children without resorting to hurtful and destructive actions.

Currently, (Name of Organization) is able to offer training in seven parent groups in (cities and counties in service area). Last year, _____ parents were enrolled in one of these groups. It is impossible to estimate how much family violence was prevented by these sessions, but we do know the impact (Name of Organization) has had on the families who have regularly been a part of the (Name) groups.

Of course, there are many more parents and children who would benefit from learning about the proven techniques that (Name of Organization) staff and volunteers teach. Violence against children is, sadly, increasing. (Name of Organization)'s proven program both stops and prevents abuse. It is limited only by resources to expand the number of parent groups and spread the news about the availability of the program.

This year, (Name of Organization) will be expanding its program into the Hispanic community as well as continuing to maintain the current number of parent groups. This is modest growth, but it demonstrates the organization's commitment to serve all affected families in the greater (location) community. This will require raising $_____ this fiscal year.

I ask that you join with me in support of this important work and give serious consideration to making a contribution of $_____. Should that increase not be possible, please send the best gift you can. Whatever you give to (Name of Organization) is an investment in the health and safety of our community.

SECOND SOLICITATION LETTER

(DATE)
Mr/Ms Full Name
1000 Good Times Lane
Your City, State (ZIP)

Dear Ms. Spotsylvania:
You and I can only imagine the anxiety experienced by those in our community who want to work, to be productive, but have obstacles that hinder them in finding and keeping a job. For some, the barrier is a lack of transportation; for others, it is a physical or mental disability. Yet, each one of them has a desire and a need to be employed.

When I wrote to you in September, I shared a part of the (Name of Organization)'s story that most of us had not heard. Every day, we provide real opportunities for our fellow citizens—through individual assessments, training, and counseling—to find and keep jobs. For some of the most severely disabled, (Name of organization) trains and employs over (#) people with disabilities in the organization's (List of Programs).

The disabled population who needs (Name of Organization)'s programs and services is rapidly growing in our region, and (Name of Organization) needs more funds to provide them with training and employment opportunities.

You and I can help close that gap. Our financial support of (Name of Organization) will enable the organization to reach more people with disabilities throughout the (cities and counties) service area.

Once again, I ask that you join with me in the financial support of (Name of Organization), and consider becoming a member of one of our Recognition Clubs with a gift of $100 or more to the (year) Annual Fund. But, whatever you can contribute will be a direct investment in the lives of people who want what we all want—the chance to work.

Sincerely,

Volunteer

Chairperson

Annual Fund Committee

YEAR-END SOLICITATION LETTER

(DATE)

Mr. and Mrs. Joseph and Mary Doe
1234 Dogwood Lane
Your City, State ZIP

Dear Joe and Mary:

As (residents, family members, etc.), we are fully aware of the high quality of life and care (we, our parents, etc.) receive at (Name of Organization) Retirement Community. Each day, staff members and volunteers help create an atmosphere of love, compassion, and community for (us, residents).

We should also be aware that the amenities that (we, family members of residents, etc.) expect and enjoy are made possible through a combination of funding sources, a growing part of which are contributed dollars from those of us who understand what a critical and positive difference (Name of Organization) makes in (our, etc.) lives.

Unlike for-profit, secular institutions, (Name of Organization) makes a life-long commitment to all who are a part of this community. Those who have served the church, those who have had severe medical problems, those who have simply outlived their resources—all are embraced by this Christian community. Our privilege and our challenge is to provide the financial support that will enable the staff to continue providing the nurturing care that has always been a hallmark of (Name of Organization).

Please join me in helping to provide the level of financial support needed by (Name of Organization) on an annual basis. I am asking that you consider a gift of $_____. In consideration of this gift, (Name of Organization) wishes to recognize you with membership in the _____ Society, a new group of supporters honoring the contributions of _____ in the development of this community. If this amount is not possible, I encourage you to make the best gift you can.

With appreciation, I send my best wishes.

Sincerely,

Volunteer

P.S. (Name of Organization)'s fiscal year ends June 30.

END OF YEAR LETTER TO TRUSTEES

(DATE)

(Inside Address)

Dear (first name):

With December 31 but a few weeks away, I thought that now would be an especially good time to remind you of the benefits of making a generous contribution to (Name of Organization) before the end of the tax year.

We who are the owners and principal leaders of (Name of Organization) know well of the pressing financial needs. This year, $_____ must be raised to close the gap between the actual cost of delivering essential services and the funds received from federal, state, and local governments. It is important to note that government programs have not increased funding in eleven years, while our costs have continued to rise.

Please join me in two ways this holiday season: 1) making a minimum gift of $1000 to the Annual Fund drive; and 2) giving serious consideration to providing a special gift of appreciated securities or property.

As Directors, our gifts are important for two reasons—one is, of course, to make available much-needed funds for the organization we serve; the other is the example we set for others to follow.

I send my best wishes to you and your family for the happiest of holidays.

Sincerely,

(Name), Chair

Board of Directors

Encl.

PARENTS LETTER

(DATE)
   (Inside Address)

   Dear (first name):
   (Name of Student), an alumna of the (Name) Ballet Company, said: "(Organization) has given me opportunities I never dreamed I would have, such as dancing the lead in *Sleeping Beauty* with a professional dancer."
   (Name of Student) is currently a dance major at (Name) College in (City), one of several young people who have been trained, nurtured, and motivated to pursue careers in dance through participation in (Name) Ballet Company.
   We who are parents of (Organization) dancers understand what (Name of Student) is saying, for we see the positive impact of the program in our children. Not all will have the talent or the desire to become professional dancers, but all are becoming more self-confident, more poised. The study of classical ballet—the discipline and hard work that is required to succeed—underscores the values we work to instill in our children.
   The operating budget for (Name) Ballet Company is $50,000. This modest amount enables the production of two full-length ballets each year, original choreography, professional guest artists, and the immeasurable positive impact on our families and our community.
   Recognizing how special (Organization) has been to our daughter, we have decided to contribute to help meet the needs of the current budget. We invite you to join us in making an annual gift in support of the program. We ask that you consider a gift of $100, but whatever you decide, we encourage you to make the best gift you can.
   (Name of Student) continued: "For me, dancing has given me much self-confidence in all I do in life. Without (Organization)'s students and staff, I know I would not have the opportunities I have today."
   In these few words, (Name of Student) has summed up the importance of (Organization) to all of us. Please, use the enclosed return envelope and send your contribution today.
   Sincerely,
   Joe and Sally Volunteer

PROOF SHEET SAMPLE

(DATE)
   Dear Friends of (Organization):
   Enclosed is a "Proof Sheet" listing those who have made a gift to ORGANIZATION since July 1, 2007. We are sending this in preparation for the **2008 Annual Report and Honor Roll of Donors**.

As the (Organization)'s fiscal year comes to a close, we'd appreciate your help with one of the following:

1. For those of you who have already stepped forward and contributed to (Organization), thank you once again! Please review the list to be sure that we have shown your name, or your company's name, the way you would like it to appear in the final printing of our **Honor Roll of Donors**. If not, please let us know.

2. If you have not yet made a contribution, **there's still time**. However, in order for your contribution to be counted and listed in this fiscal year, we must receive it by **June 30**.

Only with your support can (Organization) continue to teach positive parenting techniques that have been shown to improve the quality of lives of the parents and children in our neighborhoods. And, safer, more affirmative families contribute to the well-being of all of us.

Thank you for your investment in our program and our communities.

Sincerely,

(Name)

Executive Director

Enclosure

PROSPECT EVALUATION FORM

Prospect:_____ Occupation: _____

Address: _____ Business: _____

Telephone (Home): _____ (Business): _____

Relationship to Organization: _____

RATING GRID

I (high)	7						
N	6						
T	5						
E	4						
R	3						
E	2						
S	1						
T (low)		$10,000	$25,000	$50,000	$100,000	$500,000	$1 Mil +

Spouse:_____

Children: _____

Spouse's Occupation: _____

Organization's Program Interests: _____

Club Memberships: _____

Board Memberships: _____

Other Philanthropic Interests: _____

Financial Information: _____

Net Worth: _____

Annual Income: _____

Salary: _____

Giving History For: _____

Year: _____

Number of Gifts: _____

Amount: _____

Cultivation Strategy Planning Form

Prospect: _____ Business Phone: _____

Address: _____ Home Phone: _____

FAX: _____

Gift Potential: Short term: $ _____ Long term: $_____

Annual Gift Goal: $ _____ Major Gift Goal: $ _____

Planned Gift Goal: $ _____

Vehicle: _____

Overall cultivation strategy for reaching goals: _____

Date	Next Step	Outcome	Staff/Volunteers

PROSPECT CALL REPORT

Prospect(s) _____   **Date of Report** _____

Place of Call:
___Prospect's Ofice
___Prospect's Home
___Telephone
___Other_____

Purpose of Call:
___Gift Request
___Recruit for Campaign
___Cultivation

Assessment of Interest:
_____ Warm _____ Cool _____ Fair _____ Negative

What Happened During the Visit?
___ Pledge made ___ Cash gift w/out pledge ___ Considering pledge
___ Refused to pledge
___Naming opportunity (describe) _____
Comments: _____
_____

What is the Recommended Next Step and by When?
_____

PLANNED GIVING ADVISORY COMMITTEE JOB DESCRIPTION

Overview

The Planned Giving Advisory Committee will establish and oversee a program that provides current, useable information to selected prospective donors about estate-planning techniques to encourage and facilitate such major gifts to the organization

Objectives

1. To encourage the inclusion of bequests in wills for the restricted and unrestricted purposes of the organization.
2. To encourage the creation of charitable trusts and the acquisition of gift annuities for restricted and unrestricted purposes.
3. To encourage the writing of life insurance where the organization is the owner and beneficiary.
4. To monitor tax laws in order to assist prospective donors in making major contributions to the institution.
5. To communicate the ways and means for donors to use securities, real estate, and other properties to make major gifts.
6. To write articles and conduct seminars for logical constituents of the organization.
7. To serve as advisors to the staff of the organization on specific, as well as general, matters related to planned giving.
8. To review and recommend policies and guidelines for the planned giving program to the board of directors.
9. To review and select the printed materials used in the planned giving program.

Committee Membership

The committee will be composed of *agents of wealth* who will not be asked to provide names of prospects nor solicit gifts. Membership should include at least one attorney, a officer, a CLU, a CPA, and a financial advisor/planner.

PLANNED GIVING PROGRAM SAMPLE ACTION PLAN

Objectives

Time Frame	Action Steps
1.___	Recruit a chairman and members of the Planned Giving Council whose purpose is to assist in establishing, overseeing, and implementing a program that identifies and informs selected individuals about estate planning techniques, to assist them in making major gifts to the institution. Membership on the committee will consist both of Agents of Wealth and tax and estate planning laypersons.
2.	Draft policies and procedures for the planned giving program to be passed by the board of trustees.
3.	Build a list, with the assistance of volunteers, of 25 planned giving prospects.
4.	Conduct a seminar on estate planning.
5.	Achieve ___ planned gift commitment(s) by the end of the fiscal year.
6.	Select and prepare to send an estate- planning newsletter to selected prospects by _____.
7.	Conduct an informational session on planned giving to members of the board(s).
8.	Schedule planned giving visits with each member of the board, asking the individual to seriously consider putting the organization in their will.

WILLS BEQUEST PROGRAM

(Name of Organization)
(Name) SOCIETY

Objectives

A wills bequest program will be conducted to:

1. Identify friends of the (Name of Organization) who have put the organization in their wills

2. Invite friends to consider putting the (Name of Organization) in their wills

3. Appropriately recognize during their lifetimes friends of the (Name of Organization) who have made estate commitments through wills and/or trusts

Materials Needed

Recognition Society brochures

Confidential reply card

Return envelope

Membership material may include:
    Membership card
    Lapel pin
    Certificate
    Plaque

Plan of Action

Projected Completion Dates	Activity
_____	1. Select three candidates who have put the organization in their wills who could serve as chair of the (Name of Organization)
_____	2. Recruit the chair, working in order of priority.

_____	3. Prepare materials for mailing:
	    a. Letter of invitation to join the (Name of Organization)
	    b. Brochure with confidential reply card
	    c. Return envelope

_____	4. Identify and prepare mailing list:
	    a. Board and former board members
	    b. Alumni (ae)/parents/clients/patients/etc.
	    c. Friends of the organization 60 years of age and older
	    d. Employees and retired employees
	    e. Other logical constituents

_____	5. Prepare/produce recognition materials
_____	6. Prepare and mail letters of invitation

_____	7. Follow-up with responses as received
	    a. Phone call
	    b. Personal visit

_____	8. Prepare and mail second letter of invitation

_____	9. Plan and implement event for members of the (Name of Organization)
	    a. Select event
	    b. Prepare invitations
	    c. Mail invitations

_____	10. Prepare article on the (Name of Organization) for the organization's newsletter

INVITATION TO JOIN PLANNED GIVING RECOGNITION SOCIETY LETTER

(DATE)
   Mr/Ms Full Name
   1000 Good Times Lane
   Your City, State (ZIP)

   Dear Name:
   It is indeed a privilege to have this opportunity to invite you to join me in participating in a new and most important recognition program at the Virginia Council of Churches—The Date Palm Society.
   The Date Palm Society provides the Virginia Council of Churches the means to recognize appropriately those who understand the importance of ecumenism and have included the Council in their estate plans. Moreover, it will serve to lift up the significance of bequest-related giving and to encourage others to make estate commitments which will help guarantee the perpetuation of the Council's vital work. Further, you may wish to establish an endowed fund in your own name, or to honor or memorialize the name of a loved one. In this manner you are assured that your gift will perpetuate your generosity and the impact it will have on ecumenism in the Commonwealth.
   I urge you to give serious consideration to your own participation in The Date Palm Society, and to join with us now to ensure that the Virginia Council of Churches will have the resources to continue to grow and to prosper.
   Sincerely,
   (Name)
   Chair
   The Date Palm Society

THE JOHN DOE ENDOWED _____ FUND

In recognition of the benefits which (Name of Organization) provides to its employees and to the (Name) community, this Endowed Fund is hereby established.
   The following will be guidelines for administration of the Fund:
   I. For investment purposes, funds contributed to and designated for the John Doe Endowed _____ Fund will be integrated into the organization's permanent endowment with other funds of the (Name of Organization's) endowment, with the understanding that the principal amount of the Fund will share equally in the growth of the endowment, and the Fund will be designated by name on the books of the organization.

II. The John Doe Endowed _____ Fund will be identified annually in the appropriate official publication of (Name of Organization).

III. Friendship Industries agrees that the John Doe Endowed _____ Fund will be activated and Doe grants awarded annually at the time the Fund reaches $25,000.

IV. Earnings on the Fund will be used for: _____
Consideration will be given to those who: _____
If these terms are not met in any given year, the organization may use the income for purposes appropriate to the mission and purpose of Friendship Industries.

V. The Fund shall be administered through procedures prescribed by the board and management of Friendship Industries.

VI. Should endowment expenditures for the stated purposes become unnecessary at some future date, the earnings may be used in support of other facets of the organization's program.

Signed:
John Doe, Donor, President
(Name of Organization)
Entered into this day of, 201_.

CAMPAIGN GIFT ACCEPTANCE POLICIES

Policies Regarding Gift Acceptance:

1. Gifts for approved campaign objectives paid or pledged between ___/___/___ and ___/___/___, including bequest distributions, will be counted in the campaign.

2. Whenever possible, unrestricted gifts will be sought for the project and recognition will be provided, according to recognition policies as approved by the board of directors. Restricted gifts will be used as designated.

3. Pledges to be paid over a period of five years or less will be fully counted. The amount to be credited to the campaign for pledges to be paid over more than five years will be determined on a case-by-case basis.

4. A signed letter of intent is required for all gifts to be counted in the campaign, except for outright gifts.

5. Irrevocable deferred commitments, such as charitable remainder trusts, may be counted in campaign totals, dependent upon minimum age requirements. Deferred and other gifts received during the campaign time frame but designated for projects other than campaign priorities will not

be counted as part of the campaign. They will, however, be reported in a separate category on fundraising reports and recognized appropriately.

6. Matching gifts will be encouraged from donors affiliated with companies (as employees or directors) which will match their gifts in any ratio to the maximum extent allowed. Matching gifts will be considered corporate contributions and the individual will be recognized as initiating the funds. Consideration may be given to including matching funds toward special recognition opportunities for individuals.

7. Publicly traded securities will be sold and credited by the value at the date of transfer for the donor and at the date of sale for the campaign totals. Closely held stock with a buy-back arrangement with the corporation may be accepted.

8. Possible gifts of real estate given outright or with a life estate contract will be discussed for acceptance or non-acceptance on a case-by-case basis. Value will be determined by outside professional assessment, according to IRS requirements. Crediting of gifts of equipment and other personal properties will be evaluated on a case-by-case basis.

9. Life insurance gifts of paid-up policies, as well as new agreements with the (Name of Organization) designated as owner and beneficiary, will be discussed. Crediting will be determined on a case-by-case basis.

10. In-kind gifts not in the project budget will be counted in the campaign total but not included in the project totals. Acceptance and crediting will be determined on a case-by-case basis.

11. Funds received as campaign gifts will be invested in line with current investment policy as overseen by the finance committee of Name of Organization board of directors.

Policies Regarding Recognition:

1. All donors of $_____ or more will be included in a final honor roll of donors produced at the end of the campaign.

2. All donors of $5,000 or more will be included in _____. Listing of names will be grouped by the contribution levels.

3. A list of special recognition opportunities will be created that will include a recognition value, or dollar value, for each opportunity. The opportunities will range from $1,000 up to $1,000,000 or more. Donors who make unrestricted campaign gifts at the designated levels will be offered the opportunity to be recognized for their gifts adjacent to the funded components. Restricted gift recognition will be provided commensurate with the gift.

4. The opportunity to select a special recognition gift will be provided to prospects as they are solicited. (Name of Organization) will reserve a special recognition opportunity in conjunction with a signed pledge form or letter of intent.

5. Names of one or more donors to a specific area will be listed on _____ outside the funded area for the life of that exhibit or gallery, for example:
   "The Meal Preparation Center Presented by the ABC Company"

6. Only in selected cases and at the gift level of $_____ or more, and for spaces expected to be permanent, will consideration be given to having the donor's name first, such as "The Smith Community Kitchen." Ideally, such gifts will include a significant designation for endowment. When desired, consideration will be given to printing a company's name in the corporate typeface.

7. All donors of $_____ and above will be invited to a variety of pre-opening events and/or galas. They will receive a special recognition thank-you item.

8. Corporate donors of $_____ and above will receive a block of complimentary invitations to a series of pre-opening events to offer to employees and/or guests.

9. Campaign donors of any size gift will be listed in a thank-you advertisement to be placed in a widely distributed local newspaper.

Volunteer Recognition Policies:

1. A thank you and recognition plaque (or other tasteful format) will list all board members who served during the tenure of the campaign will be displayed.

2. A special thank you and pre-opening event will be offered to all current and former board of directors and Campaign Committee volunteers.

3. All current and former board of directors and Campaign Committee members will receive a block of complimentary invitations to a pre-opening event to share with friends and family.

(Name of Campaign)

July 1, 20 _____ to _____, _____

GIFTS AND PLEDGES BY SOURCE

Sources	# of Donors for the month	Pledges/Cont. for the month	Total # of Donors	Total Commitments
Board of Directors				
Parents of Clients				
Family Members of Clients				
Friends				
Corporations/ Businesses				
Churches, Clubs, and organizations				

Private Foundations			
Government (Fed, State, Local)			
Totals			

GIFTS AND PLEDGES BY SIZE

In the Range of	# of Donors Needed	Total Needed	# of Donors to Date	Amt Received to Date	Cumulative Total
$500,000	1	$500,000			
$250,000	2	$500,000			
$100,000	5	$500,000			
$ 50,000	10	$500,000			
$ 25,000	15	$375,000			
$ 10,000	30	$300,000			
$ 5,000	50	$250,000			
$ 1,000	100	$100,000			
Under $1,000	Many	$275,000			$3,300,000

CAPITAL CAMPAIGN PHASES

A. **Readiness Phase.** This will accomplish three major tasks: Evaluation, Planning (campaign goals and methods), and Communication. The evaluation will determine campaign readiness in these specific areas:
   1. Evaluation—to determine campaign readiness in the following areas:
      a. Board understanding and commitment
      b. Senior management support
      c. Development personnel and training
      d. Support staff
      e. Methods to determine needs and build ownership
      f. Volunteer leadership availability
      g. Donor potential
      h. Community capabilities and perceptions
      i. Other factors that will impact the campaign
      j. To study or not to study?
   2. Planning—to determine campaign goals, build ownership of key major prospects, and develop the structure needed to launch the campaign.
      a. Campaign planning
         1. Strategic planning committee or special campaign planning committee

   2. Either approach should have broad-based membership
   3. Set time line for report
   b. Campaign structure and leadership
      1. Selecting and recruiting the campaign chair
      2. Drafting and finalizing the case for support
      3. Campaign plan, including broadening ownership of the goals among other major prospects
      4. Campaign organization
      5. Selecting and recruiting members of the campaign steering committee
      6. Gift chart preparation and prospect evaluation (rating)
      7. Pledge/gift records, acknowledgment, and recognition
      8. Evaluation procedures
      9. Campaign plan, structure, and tentative time line approval
   3. Communication—to inform and build consensus among key constituencies of the need, case for support, and goals for the campaign through individual meetings and focus groups.
      a. Current and former board members
      b. Internal constituencies
      c. Major prospects
      d. Corporate leadership
      e. Other persons and groups particular to your institution

B. **Quiet Phase.** This will accomplish three major tasks: 1) Solicitation of leadership gifts (including board members); 2) Finalizing the nature and scope of the campaign; and 3) Preparing for the public phase.
   1. Solicitation of leadership gifts—to secure in gifts and pledges a minimum of 60% of the campaign goal prior to the public announcement. *This is a standard percentage prior to announcement that may be moved upward when we gain a greater understanding of your constituency.*
      a. Board members (100% participation is critical)
      b. Leadership gift prospects
   2. Finalizing the organization of the campaign
      a. Campaign steering committee meetings
      b. Securing and training other volunteer leadership
      c. Reporting procedures established
      d. Leadership gift solicitation and follow-up completed
      e. Evaluation of leadership gift results and finalization of campaign goals
      f. External communication components scheduled
   3. Preparing for the public phase—to schedule and prepare materials necessary to announce and implement the public phases of the capital campaign.
      a. Schedule and plan the public announcement
      b. External communication components finalized
      c. Volunteer solicitors for special gifts recruited and trained

C. **Public Phase** The campaign will be announced to the general public, planned communications pieces will be distributed, closure and completion of the campaign will occur.
   1. Special event to announce the campaign
      a. Media kits distributed
      b. External case appropriately distributed
   2. Systematic reporting of results through campaign newsletters and press releases
   3. Continuing evaluation and solicitation of prospects
      a. Individuals
      b. Corporate
      c. Foundations
   4. Closure and completion of the campaign
      a. Completion of solicitation efforts
      b. Evaluation of the campaign
      c. Celebration and recognition event
      d. Media announcement

SAMPLE FOUNDATION PROPOSAL LETTER

DATE
   Name
   Title
   Foundation/Corporation
   Address
   City, State, ZIP

   Dear NAME:
   This is a request to the officers of the (Foundation/Corporation) for consideration of a grant of $_____ to (Organization) for the purpose of assisting in the (construction of; funding of; building the; etc.) the (Name of Project). The total cost of the project will be $_____.
   In reviewing this proposal, the officers of the (Foundation/Corporation) may wish to note the following points:

   1.

   2.

   3.

   The following pages describe this project and programs of the which it is designed to further.

The mission of (Organization) is to provide (here describe the mission, who is served, programs, etc. Then state the needs that the organization is trying to fulfill, make a distinct contribution, and define the subject relevant to the project for which funding is being sought.)

(Describe the project, what it is, why it is needed now, and what its completion will enable the organization to achieve. Place it in the context of the campaign/current fundraising program. Talk in positive terms: "We are doing thus and so—but we need to do this and that to serve a growing number of students etc.")

(Next, talk about the specific qualifications of the organization to be carrying on this work [strengths, character/nature of the students/other persons being served/wanting service, faculty, etc.]) Discuss the planning that underlies the project.

(Review the requirements to realize the project. Include financial projections and how the new facility/program/endowment will be maintained following completion. Provide information on funding from other sources that will give the Foundation/Corporation reason to believe that its funds will be well placed)

(Conclude by underscoring the project's importance and the impact a grant from the Foundation/Corporation will have on the organization's ability to carry out its mission.)

Enclosures (based on the Foundation/Corporation's requirements):

Institutional facts (brief history, philosophy, physical and financial resources, enrollment)

Material that supports the proposal (staff resumes, publications, etc.)

Listing of board members with positions and names of companies/firms

List of administrative offices

Recent audit

Nonprofit status as provided by IRS

NOTE: Provide exactly what the Foundation or Corporation requires—nothing more and nothing less.

CHAPTER 7

Research and Recordkeeping

Many years ago at the Chautauqua Institute in New York, a number of development newcomers and some old-timers were introduced to a consummate professional in the field of records and reports. In the course of a day, the late Rene Hoyle had presented more details about the proper way to set up and run the record-keeping system in a development office than one brain could contain. Since that time in the early 1970s, her lessons have been learned, adapted, changed, and added to. But that firm beginning—and initial information overload—has served very well over the years. It is from that knowledge base that this chapter will be built.

"MAKE THE JUICE WORTH THE SQUEEZE"

The title comes from a good West Virginia friend and colleague who applied that test to nearly everything he did both personally and professionally. It is a bit of country wisdom from which we can all benefit. However you choose to handle the data that comes into your development office, you must be concerned about the cost/benefit ratio of how you and (if you have them) others on your staff spend time and money. To be the most productive, you should apply your awareness of diminishing returns to the prospect identification effort, depth of research, clerical priorities, prospect information form design, and data base size. A small staff should concentrate on the relatively small number of prospective donors of major gifts. Highly detailed records, for example, may appear impressive, but are warranted only for board members and major prospects.

Here, then, are the considerations to keep in mind when setting up or analyzing your system of keeping records:

- The system should facilitate the identification of major prospects and supply pertinent information on each of them.

- In addition to computer records, hard-copy files on board members, volunteers, and major prospects (lifetime and estate-related) should be maintained for letters, hand-written notes, and other visual materials. In this computer age, it is possible to scan materials into computer files, but it is wise to keep these actual documents in a file drawer.

- The system should ensure that it is relatively simple to retrieve the data in the format that will assist you in your work. Whatever computer program you use, it must enable the generation of lists that may be sorted in a developmentally useful way (by gift size, geographic area, class year, et al.).

- The system should enable the processing of pledges and gifts so that a letter or other appropriate acknowledgement can be sent in a timely manner. The rule of thumb is that a thank-you letter should be sent no later than three days after the gift is received.

- The system should enable you to produce reports that measure progress and that are understandable to staff and volunteers. The best system, research, and records are absolutely valueless unless your CEO, board members, other key volunteers, and staff use the material. The fanciest, most detailed reports, for example, may do more to confuse than inform. Make certain that the reports and other forms provided for those who must use them are easily understood and will help them achieve your organizational funding goals.

Remember that research and record keeping are a part of the development process, not the end product. The primary goal of any system should be to facilitate the raising of funds your organization needs. Research and records identify signposts that point to where potential funds may be sought and can suggest the methods to use in approaching the suspects and prospects.

There are a number of database programs available to nonprofits today to record gifts and other important information. Some very effective and comprehensive ones are available online and may be rented rather than purchased so that powerful development tools may be affordable to organizations with small budgets. The objective should be an efficient central records system that does away with useless duplication of files, records, and efforts with complete and useable information in one location available to all authorized staff members.

Online programs, in particular, can accommodate a number of users so that information can be entered and shared by those who are involved in the cultivation and solicitation process. Two of the most prominent of these online services with which we are familiar are:

- DonorPerfect Online (www.donorperfect.com)
- eTapestry (www.etapestry.com)

Both of these are available for a monthly subscription fee that is dependent upon the number of records and modules your organization wishes to utilize. They are as powerful and secure as any program that an organization might purchase, and they are constantly being upgraded to make certain the software meets customers' needs. In the case of eTapestry, a small nonprofit with less than 500 names on its list can use very basic aspects of the program at no charge.

These comments are not to suggest that these online options are better than development software packages that are offered for sale; it is only to suggest that your organization may be able to access powerful database tools that will enable you to work smarter and better than the current Excel spreadsheet enables.

If you utilize web-based database systems, do not expect your volunteers to interact easily or willingly with these programs, regardless of the training and assurances that they are provided. There will be less frustration all around if volunteers are shown a simple spreadsheet listing their prospects, contact information, objectives, deadlines, results, and recommended next steps. Putting this document on Google Docs and sharing it with the appropriate individuals is about as "high tech" as we would advise you to get.

Simplicity is important to keep volunteers and development staff members up-to-date on the progress being made, and the next steps to be taken with individual prospects. You can keep—and must keep—more complete records in the main database system, but do not expect your volunteers to be of help.

Where Am I, And What Do I Do?

Whether your development office has one person or 30+, the same principles apply: Start from where you are—people, materials, and equipment. Yours is not the only organization with incomplete records and/or an inadequate internal system of recordkeeping and reporting. Do not allow the past to dictate the future; however, use what has occurred to build the foundation for a better system.

Begin by charting the current path of prospect data and gifts from the entry point in the office to the computer and hard-copy files. Include the generation of acknowledgement letters, financial reports, etc. This will promote a thorough comprehension of existing procedures, files, forms, staffing, and problem areas. Sometimes, a flow chart can help simplify the process. Meet with staff members and with those in related offices to get information, and obtain a consensus among those who will be interacting with the system. Also, obtain the input and support of the CEO, the chief financial officer, the board development committee chair, and the chief development officer. Everyone who interacts with the development records should be convinced that the system will produce the information needed in a timely and useable way. After you have drafted the re-designed system, meet again with those who will be using it to get their input and agreement before finalizing the process. Make certain that the applicable business office staff member is a part of the process and understands and accepts the system you will be using. Avoid frustration by involving the business office while the system is being created—not after decisions have been made. Once completed, place the written description of the system, along with forms and other related materials, in the development office manual.

The objective is to provide an understandable road map that any staff member can follow. The result of your efforts should be a central records office and integrated system—accepted and implemented.

THE CONTINUING PROCESS OF EVALUATING AND PLANNING

When the new or revised system is in place, your work is still not done. It would be very unusual for any system to be perfect from the time it is put into operation. The following six suggestions will help you refine your recordkeeping system and improve its ability to serve the development program:

1. Use regular meetings to serve as checkpoints regarding progress toward agreed-upon goals and to identify problem areas.

2. Set deadlines for reports that are realistic considering resources currently available.

3. Schedule wisely so that peak workloads are reduced.

4. Establish regular opportunities (meetings, report forms) for prospect feedback from staff and volunteers to flow into the records system.

5. Foster an attitude of shared responsibility for accurate records among staff.

6. Continually evaluate techniques, costs, and benefits of data maintenance, as well as initial data collection.

The work of maintaining accurate telephone numbers, recent addresses, and job changes, and other pertinent information about your board members, significant volunteers, and major prospects is never-ending. The task will require a number of techniques from simply asking someone about someone else, to the design and use of annual fund gift return envelopes. Successful development professionals make the process of data gathering a natural part of the daily process of doing their jobs, cultivating listening skills, asking appropriate questions, and remembering what is heard until they can write it down.

GENERAL PRINCIPLES OF PROSPECT IDENTIFICATION, RESEARCH, AND RATING

Now that you have an effective method of keeping records and generating needed reports, the information gathered on prospects can be efficiently and productively utilized. However, conducting research can be the most difficult task in any development office. There are few organizations that can employ someone for that purpose. Normally, the task falls to the development staff members who, in many small organizations, may be one person. Yet, building a major prospect list and gathering information about each person thereon are essential in raising the funds to meet your organization's needs. Here are some principles that will help guide your efforts:

- Be rational in your approach to your prospect list. Do not let your list just grow; control it through consideration of the relevant variables of your organization, your solicitation methods, the number of your prospects, geographic area covered, and the funding goal. Some of the factors are the:
  - Financial ability of the prospect
  - Interest in and relationship each has with your organization
  - Accessibility of the prospect to volunteers and staff members
  - Frequency and amounts of previous giving
  - Number of dependents and whether dependents are already financially secure
  - Age of the prospect—older persons are preferable if wealth is equivalent
  - Connection with a board member or key volunteer.
- Recognize the needs of people to give—their motivations—including:
  - Egotism and prestige
  - Family background and interests
  - Demonstrated competence or seeker of power
  - Emotional response to death of family member
  - Sense of loyalty
  - Altruism
- Research prior major donors to your organization.
- Seek the help of your governing and auxiliary boards:
  - Ask each board member to fill out an information form and provide a biography.
  - Find out about relatives, friends, family backgrounds, special interests, church, civic and political activities, and membership in prestigious clubs.
- Identify and research other known friends of major donor potential, such as:

- Former board members and their widows/widowers
- Descendants of organization's founder(s) or early major donors
- Prominent alumni(ae) or members of constituent organizations
- Board members of competing organizations in your immediate area. Know if the primary allegiance of your prospect is elsewhere.
- Wealthy parents of students, alumni(ae) or clients

- Solicit the personal knowledge of board members, staff members, and prominent supporters (The best source of information):
  - Prepare lists for review by well-informed volunteers—in a rating committee or individually.
  - Create an easy-to-use form for rating.
  - Investigate in-house lists and those of other organizations—e.g., suppliers, museum memberships, prominent church layperson lists, etc.

IN SUMMARY

Organizations large and small need accurate records kept in ways that facilitate their ability to work with clients, students, parents, grateful patients, and other donors and prospects. Information truly is powerful because it enables CEOs and development officers to work more efficiently and effectively. Good systems also give confidence to those who interact with the information and have informed and involved everyone who must participate for the process to work smoothly.

While you may be tempted to make excuses for not gathering pertinent information about your key constituents, this task is as important as anything else you do in raising friends and funds for your organization. Lack of budget should not be a deterrent — using volunteers (board members and others) to suggest and give information about prospects, acquiring new prospects through a prospect identification program, and one-on-one visits with your organization's good friends will reap a bounty of useful data that can be the basis for building and maintaining a healthy database of major prospects.

DONOR RECOGNITION POLICY[1]

Policies Regarding Recognition:

1. All donors of $_____ or more will be included in a final honor roll of donors produced at the end of the (fiscal year) (campaign).

---

[1] Morris, Patricia S., MPA, CFRE—This document may be used by any organization as a basis for building a new or revised policy.

2. All donors of $____ or more will be included in _____.
   A listing of names will be grouped by the contribution levels.

3. A list of special recognition opportunities will be created that will include a recognition value, or dollar value, for each opportunity. The opportunities will range from $_____ up to $_____ or more. Donors who make unrestricted gifts at the designated levels will be offered the opportunity to be recognized for their gifts adjacent to the funded components. Restricted gift recognition will be provided commensurate with the gift.

4. The opportunity to select a special recognition gift will be provided to prospects as they are solicited. (The Organization) will reserve a special recognition opportunity in conjunction with a signed pledge form or letter of intent.

5. Names of one or more donors to a specific area will be listed on _____ outside the funded area for the life of that exhibit or gallery, for example: "The Client Center Presented by the ABC Company"

6. Only in selected cases and at the a gift level of $_____ or more, and for spaces expected to be permanent will consideration be given to having the donor's name first, such as "The Donor Name Building." Ideally, such gifts will include a significant designation for endowment. When desired, consideration will be given to printing a company's name in the corporate typeface.

7. All donors of $_____ and above will be invited to a variety of pre-opening events and/or galas. They will receive a special recognition thank-you item.

8. Corporate donors of $_____ and above will receive a block of complimentary invitations to a series of pre-opening events to offer to employees and/or guests.

9. Campaign donors of any size gift will be listed in a thank-you advertisement to be placed in a widely distributed local newspaper.

Volunteer Recognition Policies:

1. A thank you and recognition (sign) (plaque) list of all volunteers who served during the tenure of the (fiscal year) (campaign) will be displayed.

2. A special thank you and (annual) (pre-opening) event will be offered to all current and former board of directors and (fiscal year) (campaign committee) volunteers.

3. All current and former board of directors and (fiscal year) (campaign committee) members will receive a block of complimentary invitations to (annual) (pre-opening) event to share with friends and family.

GIFT ACCEPTANCE POLICIES[2]

(The Organization) shall accept only those gifts, the transfer and ownership of which are not inconsistent with any applicable laws or public policy, that will enable the organization to further its mission, goals, purposes, and services.

Any officer or director of (The Organization) shall be authorized to accept on behalf of the (The Organization) any unrestricted gift of cash or marketable securities.

Whenever possible, unrestricted gifts will be sought and recognition will be provided according to recognition policies as approved by the board of directors. Restricted gifts will be used as designated.

A signed pledge card or letter of intent is required for all gifts to be counted in a campaign (annual, endowment, planned giving, capital) except for outright gifts.

Matching gifts will be encouraged from donors affiliated with companies (as employees, retirees, or directors) that will match their gifts in any ratio to the maximum extent allowed. Matching gifts will be considered corporate contributions and the individual will be recognized as initiating the funds.

Gift items of tangible personal property such as furniture, works of art, and office equipment, may be accepted by the CEO on behalf of (The Organization). Gift items such as automobiles, airplanes, and boats are discouraged and may be accepted only with the prior approval of the executive committee.

Gifts of real estate given outright or with a life estate contract may be accepted by any officer but only with the prior approval of the executive committee. Value will be determined by outside professional assessment, according to IRS requirements. This assessment must be provided by the donor. Crediting of gifts of equipment and other personal properties will be evaluated on a case-by-case basis.

Gifts of life insurance policies may be accepted by any officer but prior approval of the executive committee shall be required if future premium payments are required to maintain the policy (unless accompanied by a pledge from the donor to contribute the necessary funds to cover the premiums). Crediting will be determined on a case-by-case basis.

In-kind gifts, through the performance of services or bargain sales to (The Organization), may be accepted by any officer or director of (The Organization) if the service or property involved is of the type that would customarily be purchased by (The Organization) in the normal course of its activities. In-kind crediting will be determined on a case-by-case basis.

Publicly traded securities will be sold and credited by the value at the date of transfer for the donor and at the date of sale for entry into (The Organization) donor records. Gifts of closely held and other non-marketable securities

[2] Morris, Patricia S., MPA, CFRE—This document may be used by any organization as a basis for building a new or revised policy.

and partnership interests are not encouraged and require prior approval of the executive committee before being accepted by any officer or director.

Gifts of other forms of property, including closely held and other non-marketable securities and partnership interests, are not encouraged and require prior approval of the executive committee before being accepted by any officer or director.

Deferred gifts through codicils, charitable remainder trusts, and other techniques are encouraged, but gift annuities, bargain sales, and other arrangements involving a financial commitment on the part of the organization require prior approval of the executive committee before being accepted by any officer.

Gifts that are accompanied by conditions, restrictions, stipulations, encumbrances, debt, or other factors that warrant careful review prior to acceptance shall be accepted only by an officer and only with the prior approval of the executive committee.

(The Organization)'s development office shall be responsible for providing executive committee members with all available relevant documentation regarding any proposed gift requiring their prior approval. Such documentation may include, but shall not be limited to, the following: (a) a completed title examination in the case of real estate; (b) an appraisal in the case of real estate, tangible personal property, non-marketable securities, or other assets for which no market value is readily ascertainable; (c) a preliminary environmental review which may be followed by an environmental engineering study if so indicated in the case of real estate; and (d) an estimate of the likely sales price and the time it may take to sell or otherwise dispose of the property if it is not to be retained by (The Organization) for its use in carrying out its charitable purposes.

(The Organization)'s development office shall see that prompt acknowledgements, thank-you letters, and other documentation are sent to all donors. Documentation shall be in such form and containing such information as may be required or suggested from time to time by the federal income tax laws, by the Internal Revenue Service, and (the Organization)'s auditors.

Funds received will be invested according to policies adopted from time to time by the finance committee of (The Organization)'s board of directors.

Organization's Gift Stewardship Policy

It is the intention of (The Organization) to be good stewards of the gifts provided for the benefit of our continued vitality. To that end, the directors will give strict attention to its fiduciary responsibility to provide conservative, strong, and consistent management of all funds entrusted to it, in accordance with the "prudent person" investment standard.

Acceptance of all gifts by (The Organization)'s staff and directors will be in accordance with the Gift Acceptance Policies. Emphasis shall be placed on preserving the value of each gift; therefore all gifts, with the exception of life insurance and annuity products, shall be converted to cash in an orderly fashion. Informed professionals may be used to assist in the disposal of items requiring specialized knowledge. Pending utilization for the purpose for which given, the net cash proceeds from all gifts, along with gifts of cash, shall, unless otherwise required by the donor, be invested in accordance with the Investment Policy, having the safeguarding of principal as the primary objective.

All gifts will be utilized only for those purposes identified by the donor and will be recognized as described by the donor of the funds.

For investment purposes, the proceeds of gifts may be commingled and grouped together with other monies. The handling of gifts shall be reviewed at least quarterly by (The Organization)'s finance committee, to ensure compliance with the purpose designated by the donor.

(The Organization)'s staff shall publish annually a report on fund activities. This report will be distributed to the board and be available to donors and other designated persons upon request.

Approved by board on (date).

INVESTMENT POLICY[3]

The three principal categories of endowment and similar funds are General Endowment funds, Restricted Endowment funds, and Funds Functioning as Endowment (Quasi-Endowment).

General Endowment Funds are funds received from a donor with the restriction that the principal is not expendable. If the donor specifies that the spendable return from the fund must to be used for a certain program or other specific purpose, the fund is a Restricted Endowment. A Fund Functioning as Endowment (Quasi-Endowment) is a fund that is established by the governing board to function like an endowment fund but may be expended at any time at the discretion of the board.

General Endowment

The finance committee of the Organization's board of directors has established this investment policy for the purpose of providing general guidelines for the prudent investment management of the General Endowment Fund's assets. It is recognized that changing economic and market conditions may make it difficult for the fund to precisely mirror all aspects of this investment policy at any point in time and, as such, this policy is to serve primarily as a general framework within which the fund is to be managed.

---

[3] Morris, Patricia S., MPA, CFRE—This document may be used by any organization as a basis for building a new or revised policy.

Authority for Implementing the Investment Policy

The finance committee can elect to delegate the investment management duties for all or some part of the General Endowment Fund to one or more professional investment manager(s), who shall be guided by the overall investment policy guidelines established by this policy statement. The investment manager(s) shall meet with the finance committee annually to review the performance of the Organization's investments.

Any direction to the investment manager to change any policy must come from the Organization finance committee.

Investment Objectives

The investment objectives of the endowment are to:

1. Maintain an endowment spending policy that protects the real value of the endowment principal, i.e., that preserves the value of the principal adjusted for inflation.

2. Maintain a proper balance between the preservation of capital and the growth of the purchasing power of endowment principal.

3. Provide a total return over the long term, which is at least 6% above inflation.

Spending Policy

Funds from the endowment will be withdrawn annually to help supplement the Organization's operating revenue. Thus it is an additional source of operating revenue. This withdrawal is based on a spending rate. Funds may also be withdrawn from the Quasi-Endowment pursuant to a Quasi-Endowment spending rate established in light of the budgeted current year withdrawals from those funds for capital expenditures and debt service. The finance committee will review the spending rate annually based on recommendations from the administration.

Asset Allocation

Asset allocation policy is a very important determinant of the rate of return achieved. Consequently, the finance committee should review its asset allocation policy targets on a regular basis. Current asset allocation ranges for investments through the investment manager are set at the following targets. These target ranges should be reviewed at least on a quarterly basis:

Investment	Range
Equities	50–75%
Fixed Income	25–50%

The investment manager shall have discretion within these overall allocations.

In addition, the Endowment shall hold contributed real estate for long-term investment prior to sale when board action so directs. Cash shall generally be limited to new gifts not yet pooled in other investment accounts.

Performance should be monitored regularly, including comparisons to appropriate indices.

Rebalancing will be needed periodically to bring the investment composition in line with the specified targets. The committee will review asset allocation quarterly and direct the fund to be rebalanced when it deems necessary.

Special Endowment

From time to time the finance committee may direct the treasurer that the Organization shall hold a given stock, bond, or other investment outright, and not as part of the managed endowment pool. Such action may be based on development or other considerations apart from general investment philosophy. Such investments shall be known in the aggregate as the Special Endowment. The treasurer shall report quarterly to the finance committee on the value and composition of the Special Endowment.

Short-Term Investments

The Organization's short-term investments are to be managed in such a way as to preserve the value of the fund's capital and meet the cash requirements of the Organization. Consistent with these goals, the committee wishes to maximize the return on these funds.

Quality and Maturity

Short-term investments shall be restricted to highly-rated debt obligations such as, but not specifically limited to, the following:

- Treasury and other federal obligations
- Federally insured obligations
- Commercial paper of A-1/P-1 rating
- Certificates of deposit with federal guarantees
- Banker's acceptances, corporate debt instruments, and repurchase agreements of a quality equal to the above instruments
- Internal loans to other Organization funds

In addition, short-term investments may be made through money market funds or mutual funds, which invest in the instruments listed above.

The maturities should ordinarily be substantially less than one year. When funds available will exceed all cash requirements for the next year, funds may be invested for a period not to exceed eighteen months.

Responsibility for the management of short-term investments within these policies shall rest with the treasurer.

Fees

Fees and administrative procedures proposed by the treasurer or the investment managers shall be subject to the review and approval of the finance committee of the board of directors.

Review

The finance committee shall periodically review this policy as needed.

Spending Policy Addendum

Endowment

The spending rate for the Restricted and Unrestricted Endowment is currently set at 5% of the rolling three-year average of the fiscal year end market value of the endowment fund. This calculation shall include recent gifts (i.e., gifts less than three years old) only for the period of time they have participated in the endowment, so they will make the appropriate pro rata contribution to the programs they are intended to support.

Investment Authority

The investment manager shall have discretion to invest and reinvest principal and income in accordance with the investment policy and objective statement.

Asset Allocation

The portfolio shall be maintained as an income fund, and as such shall invest in short-term fixed income instruments issued by governments, municipalities, financial institutions, and corporations.

BUSINESS SUPPORT POLICIES

For the purposes of these guidelines, business support refers to any support, financial or in-kind, philanthropic or driven by marketing, advertising, and/or public relations, provided by a business (corporation, partnership, agency, family business, etc.), regardless of the nature and value of the benefit provided by (ORG), and/or the tax implications of the relationship. The term (ORG)-business relationship refers to any business support arrangement, which may benefit both entities, directly or indirectly, or be categorized as a donation.

The (ORG)'s current business model requires a diverse base of funding and partnership support from its community of constituents. This support, both cash and in-kind, includes local, state, and national business and industry organizations.

It is (ORG)'s goal to build mutually beneficial and sustainable long-term partnerships with its contributors. To facilitate that process, the (ORG) has set forth policies that enable it to comply with Federal, state, and local law, and to provide assurance to its public that (ORG)'s work to fulfill its mission includes appropriate ethical practices.

Delineation of Process and Fulfillment of Obligations

It is the responsibility of the board of directors, the chief executive officer and the chief development officer to identify and develop business support. Consideration of (ORG)'s available human and financial resources must be a part of all decisions to enter into a relationship with a contributor, as well as be sufficient to fulfill its obligations in any (ORG)-business relationship.

Potential Conflict of Interest

A conflict of interest refers to any situation in which a decision-maker—such as a board member, board officer, committee member or staff member—is influenced in an organizational decision by personal, financial, business or other concerns that are unrelated to, or in conflict with, the organization's best interest.

Statement of Policy

- No (ORG) board or staff member shall use his or her position, or the knowledge gained by virtue of that position, in a manner that conflicts with the best interests of (ORG). Each member has a duty to place the interest of (ORG) first in any dealings with or on behalf of (ORG).

- The conduct of personal business between any board or staff member and (ORG) is prohibited absent the express approval of the (ORG) executive committee/board of directors.

- Board/staff members may not obtain for themselves, their relatives, friends, and business associates, a material interest of any kind by virtue of their association with (ORG) absent the express approval of the (ORG) executive committee/board of directors.

- If a board or staff member has a material interest in a proposed transaction or in any entity involved in the transaction, or holds a position of trust, including director or officer in any such entity, he or she must make full disclosure of this interest before any discussion or negotiation of the transaction and must rescue him/herself from the vote.

- Any board member who is aware of a potential conflict of interest, with respect to any matter coming before the board or a committee of the board, shall disclose the potential conflict of interest before participating in any discussion or negotiation of any matter implicating such conflict of interest.

Exclusions

(ORG) may exclude partnerships with businesses and organizations whose practices have been identified publicly as unethical, illegal, or otherwise potentially harmful to (ORG)'s public image in the sole discretion of the board.

Business Use of (ORG) Names and Logos

(ORG) will permit the use of its logo and the name "(ORG)" on a case-by-case basis only. The CEO and CDO must approve all agreed-upon uses of name and logo, and all policies for protecting intellectual property must be adhered to. (ORG)'s name or logo may not be used as an endorsement for business, and any use must conform to the guidelines of the Internal Revenue Service Taxation of Tax-Exempt Organizations' Income from Corporate Sponsorship regulations, effective April 25, 2002.

Business Promotion of the (ORG)-Business Relationship

Businesses and organizations may promote the relationship with (ORG) in its marketing, advertising and public relations activities, providing that the activities conform to the guidelines of the Internal Revenue Service Taxation of Tax-Exempt Organizations' Income from corporate sponsorship regulations, effective April 25, 2002. In no case may a business or organization state publicly that (ORG) endorses its products or services. The CEO and CDO must approve any promotion of this business relationship.

Recognition

(ORG) will recognize business and organization support, according to standards assigned for the level of support, and will conform to the published list of donor benefits during (ORG)'s current fiscal year. Based on level of support, recognition might include signage in the (ORG), logo or listing in paid advertisements and quarterly newsletter, on the (ORG) website and where applicable, on invitations and collateral-printed materials.

Exclusive Arrangements

(ORG) will not enter into a relationship with a business or organization that restricts the (ORG) from receiving support from the business or organization's competitors, nor from using a competitor's products or services.

Support from a (ORG) Vendor

Any current or potential relationship between (ORG) and a vendor providing goods or services is not contingent upon a contribution from the vendor, although (ORG) may solicit in-kind goods and services during cost negotiations. (ORG) may also solicit (ORG) vendors for cash contributions in the normal course of business and industry fundraising as long as contracts with (ORG) are not contingent upon a vendor's gift.

Documentation

All documents relating to (ORG) business/organization relationships are a matter of record and will be maintained in the permanent donor files of (ORG)'s development office. All gift records (both cash and in-kind pledges and receipts) will be maintained in the donor database. All records will be maintained according to established policy on access to information.

Application of Policy

When agreements are applicable, they are provided by sponsor, edited and negotiated by (ORG), then signed by CEO or CDO, depending on the nature of agreement.

The donor benefits package is created at the beginning of each fiscal year and becomes the official document that lists the parameters for donor recognition.

At our request, sponsors forward (ORG) their logos at the beginning of each event, so their permission is gained and our approval is inherent in this process. Discussions between the sponsor and CDO determine the agreed-upon placement.

(ORG) will draft, if applicable, an agreement with the donor on the category, scope and term of any exclusivity arrangement.

(ORG) may cancel an agreement without advance notice if the business or organization engages in an activity that is counter to the (ORG)'s policy and mission; if the business or changes in ownership, products, or services cause the agreement to be inconsistent with the (ORG)'s mission, standards, values, and reputation, or is not in the best interest of the community the (ORG) serves; and in the event of inability of either party to carry out its responsibilities as outlined in the agreement due to unforeseen circumstances. In any case of cancellation of agreement, (ORG) will submit in writing, a signed document, approved by legal counsel if required.

Legal, Tax, and Accounting Issues

(ORG) will comply with applicable state and local laws as well as the body of general legal principles regarding solicitation, acceptance, and use of business support, including contributions.

(ORG) will comply with applicable federal, state, and local tax laws, paying particular attention to IRS corporate sponsorship regulations. (ORG) is aware that the structure of its (ORG)-business/organization relationships might determine the taxability of the resulting income, and appropriate tax reporting of exempt and taxable income is mandatory.

(ORG) will comply with the special tax rules that prohibit individuals or businesses from inappropriately benefiting from the (ORG)-business/organization relationship, as well as the general tax rules governing charitable contributions and business support.

All accounting activity within the (ORG)-business/organization relationship will comply with generally accepted accounting principles relating to accounting and crediting of revenue, including contributions.

(ORG) will respond to all public and media inquiries about its support from business and organizations, including allegations of unethical behavior, with a prompt, full, and frank discussion of the issue, the institution's actions, and the rationale for such actions.

(ORG) will avoid agreeing to requests for anonymity where such anonymity conceals a conflict of interest, real or perceived, or raises other ethical concerns.

Approved by the board of directors on ___/___/___.

SUMMARY OF CONTRIBUTIONS

July 1, 20___ through _____ ___, 20___

	Current Year	Previous Year
Total Number of Donors		
Current Operations——Cash		
Undesignated		
Designated		
Endowment		
Cash		
Securities		
Real Estate		
Government Grants		
Total—All Sources		

SUMMARY OF CONTRIBUTIONS BY SOURCE

July 1, 20___ through _____ ___, 20___

Source	Current Year		Previous Year	
	Donors	Amount	Donors	Amount
Trustees				
Directors				
Parents				
Friends				
Churches				
Clubs, Organizations				
Special Events				
United Way				
Local Businesses				
Corporations				
Private Foundations				
Government				
Other				
Total—All Sources				

CHAPTER 8

The Organization and Use of Volunteers

Our country experienced a devastating attack on September 11, 2001—on our fellow citizens and our way of life. At the time, there was shock, then anger, and, finally, resolve. Americans came together focused on working through the devastation and finding the strength to repair the damage while beginning to defeat a common enemy.

In August 2005, the Gulf Coast of the United States was severely damaged by a hurricane called Katrina. There were televised images of our countrymen and women on rooftops surrounded by water, homes completely wiped out by wind and floods, and the shocked and helpless looks of the countless persons who were displaced by this natural tragedy.

More recently in our hemisphere, the already destitute country of Haiti suffered further desolation because of a major earthquake. In a short time thereafter, Chile was hit by an even larger earthquake that threatened the west coast and Pacific islands with tsunamis.

Because we are Americans, it was not surprising that in these man-caused and natural disasters we immediately found ways to volunteer our time, energy, talents, and money to attempt to save lives, heal the wounded, and aid the survivors in rebuilding their lives. This has been a trademark of America from the beginning of our country. We do not wait for government or some other entity to respond to human needs — we find individual and collective ways to do it ourselves. That is one of our greatest national strengths and largely defines our national character.

In 1830, Alexis de Tocqueville observed:

> These Americans are the most peculiar people in the world. You'll not believe it when I tell you how they behave. In a local community, in their country, a citizen may conceive of some need which is not being met. What does he do?

He goes across the street and discusses it with his neighbor. Then what happens? A committee comes into being, and then the committee begins to function on behalf of the need. You won't believe this, but it's true; all of this is done by private citizens on their own initiative.

No organization can effectively serve its constituency without a cadre of individuals who believe in its mission and who will work without financial compensation to enable it to reach its greatest potential. Dedicated volunteers are the daily heroes in American life.

WHY DO WE VOLUNTEER?

The reasons that Americans volunteer for any organization or cause are as numerous as there are volunteers. The one constant factor is that people volunteer when it meets their needs, whatever those needs may be. Each of us is motivated to serve when the task to be accomplished helps us achieve our individual goals.

Understanding that simple concept is essential for those of us who must recruit, train, and work with volunteers. Napoleon Bonaparte understood very well that to get what he wanted, he had to find out what his men needed and assist them in getting it. If his soldiers were hungry, he promised food if they won the battle. If they were discouraged, he spoke to their pride and devotion to family and country. Winning the conflict would allow them to return home with honor.

We, too, will experience the greatest success in achieving our goals when we are able to relate them to fulfilling the needs of those whose help we must have to do so. This is fundamental to motivating others and a central component of organizational success.

WHAT VOLUNTEERS BRING TO YOUR ORGANIZATION

Anyone who has worked with volunteers for even a brief period of time has probably asked the question: "Can't I just do it myself rather than spend valuable time getting a volunteer to do it? It is hard work to recruit, train, and motivate volunteers. Some volunteers are consistently unavailable when you need them, you have to stay on their backs, and often they do not know enough to be helpful. What's more, they are habitually unreliable." You may say this—if only to yourself.

If the above describes your feelings, review how your volunteers have been selected, recruited, and trained. To paraphrase Shakespeare, "The problem may not be in our volunteers (our stars), but in ourselves." Great care should be taken in matching the right person with the task to be accomplished. Further, make certain that the individual is given sufficient training, information, and staff support so that the volunteer feels confidence in his or her ability to accomplish the task. No one should be expected to do anything that the person does not feel comfortable doing. Without that necessary level of comfort with the task, it is unlikely to be done no matter how many promises the volunteer makes or the number of nagging contacts made by you or other staff members.

No organization can hire enough staff members to do all that volunteers can do—and do more effectively—when they are properly selected, trained, and motivated. Volunteers can:

- **Extend the influence and credibility of your organization.** The stature of the people whom you recruit to serve on your boards and other important committees send signals to the public about the quality of your nonprofit and the validity of its needs.

- **Multiply the number and effectiveness of contacts for potential giving and influence**. There is a growing trend on the part of some nonprofits to hire as many major gifts officers as they can afford and diminish the use of key volunteers. While it is always important to have a staff member serve on the major giving team, it is unwise to send signals to members of the board and others with resources and influence that they are essentially "off the hook"—staff members will make the calls without the need for their significant involvement in the process. No organization can hire enough staff members or people with influence to develop the relationships and raise the funds needed to meet your goals. The right volunteer can open doors to prospects that no hired staff member could approach. Further, it is unhealthy for nonprofits to excuse their chief advocates from involvement in the development process.

- **Be your goodwill ambassadors** by helping people, groups, and communities better understand, accept, and appreciate the work of your organization.

- **Provide expert advice and an outside viewpoint on your development efforts and your organization's service.** If you let them—and show them respect for their insights and opinion—volunteers can give you a fresh look at your organization.

- **Keep you in touch with the perceptions of your organization** in the communities and groups to which you relate.

- **Assist in learning about and putting down damaging rumors.** This requires that there is a proactive effort to keep your volunteers informed. Encourage them to insist on being kept up-to-date. A trusting partnership with your volunteers will help your nonprofit keep and build a good reputation.

It should be no surprise that your volunteers are often your best donors. You have given them the opportunity to be productively involved. They have become owners with you in your organization's mission and the expression of it through your program of service.

METHODS FOR DEVELOPING VOLUNTEER INVOLVEMENT AND LEADERSHIP

Developing your program for individuals to become involved with your organization must be an active part of your annual plan. Organizations tend to have too few rather than too many opportunities for the appropriate involvement of volunteers. As we have stated in previous chapters, the key is to build an increasing level of ownership of individuals of your nonprofit's mission and goals. In selecting volunteers, as in identifying major prospects, the question is: Who owns your organization's mission and goals—or who would own them—if they knew more about them? If ownership is felt by only the inside group who make all the plans and all of the decisions, then the organization will have trouble getting the support of others beyond that inner circle.

The first step in creating or strengthening your volunteer structure is to review your current program. In conducting this review, consider whether each existing committee offers a volunteer meaningful participation. People like to know that what they are being asked to do is truly important and appropriate to their abilities, interests, and levels of influence. Is the involvement appropriate to their status in the community? Are there levels of opportunities so that a volunteer can effectively move up through ranks toward trusteeship? Is the involvement fluff or substance for you and the volunteer? Next, expand or add committees as may be appropriate, making certain that each committee's role and that of its members are clear with written job descriptions. Volunteers do require attention, so you must be able to give each group adequate staff support.

We have listed the typical fundraising, strategic planning, and marketing/communications committees in previous chapters, and will discuss thoroughly governing boards in the following chapter. In addition to these, let us suggest some other possible methods for enabling individuals to become engaged with your organization.

- **CEO's Board of Advisors.** This is sometimes called the trustee/director "Board in Waiting" or "Junior Board." Having this organized group enables you to recognize the acumen of key individuals and make use of their knowledge and influence. Some boards are organized similarly to the governing board with committees that deal with finance, program, buildings and grounds, and so on. with members assigned according to their knowledge and ability. Though such boards are advisory, they must regularly be asked for their counsel and given assurances that their advice is taken seriously by the governing board. They should be given financial, fundraising, public relations, and program issues to react to and make recommendations to be shared with the CEO who conveys their thinking to the governing board.

- **Departmental Advisory Committees.** Usually these are staffed by a member of the development department and the head of the department being advised. For a college, this could mean recruiting an advisory group for the accounting department made up of CPAs and others whose work is relevant to the profession. With the aid of such a committee, the curriculum can be reviewed in light of current practices and challenges that will benefit the faculty and better prepare students for their future careers. The development office also benefits from the ownership of a significant group of professionals investing their time and talent in the college.

    While the above example is from higher education, other organizations can use this technique as well to improve their levels of service and create opportunities for practicing professionals to become productively involved with the nonprofit.

- **Alumni(ae) Associations and Boards.** These leadership groups of alumni associations are an old standby for colleges and schools. However, other organizations have alumni(ae), too, who should not be overlooked and given the chance to continue their involvement with your organization. An organization that provides training of any productive sort will have "graduates" who have benefitted and would enjoy a way to continue their involvement. Examples of these are nonprofits in metropolitan areas that provide a safe haven, activities, and life lessons to countless children. When these youngsters become adults, many of them may very well be interested in a kind of alumni(ae) association that will give them opportunities to recall their experiences and help those current members who need what these important nonprofits provide.

Add to these anniversary committees, parents' advisory committees, and others that are appropriate for your organization. The point is actively to think of ways to get people involved with your organization in ways that are meaningful to them and important to the health of your nonprofit, now and for the long term.

SELECTING THE RIGHT PERSON
FOR THE JOB

Proceed with caution should be the motto of every development officer in selecting volunteers. The more care you take before making a commitment, the fewer problems you should have later.

For each volunteer task, create a job description that includes the skills, time commitment, etc. that will be required for the volunteer to have the best chance of success. Then, find out as much as you can about the pool of potential volunteers so that the correct choice is made for the task at hand. Here are some important questions to ask yourself in evaluating a potential volunteer. Does the prospective volunteer:

- Have the knowledge and ability for the assignment?
- Have a relationship with your organization in keeping with the task (e.g., an alumnus(a) for the job of class agent)?
- Have influence within the group he or she will be soliciting, chairing, et al.?
- Have a good or better reputation in his or her chosen profession, religious community, secular community, or your organization?
- Have a giving history with your nonprofit at a credible level for the assignment?
- Have good work habits and a well-honed sense of responsibility?
- Have a good understanding and appreciation of your organization and its mission?

Not every person will possess all of the qualities listed (plus others that may be required for a specific job), but you should be aware of the potential weaknesses as well as strengths. Thus prepared, you will make your determination realistically and will be ready to compensate for any anticipated shortcomings.

EXTENDING THE INVITATION

The process of inviting a person to serve your organization should be special, serious, and informed. It is not always necessary for a face-to-face meeting with the proposed volunteer. That would depend upon the nature of the assignment and the level of responsibility required. In every case, however, these considerations should guide your process:

- Be certain the right person on your development team does the asking. Be wary of overkill (having the CEO recruit a class agent, for example). The person asking should make the prospective volunteer feel the importance of the assignment.

- Be clear what is expected and the duration of the assignment. Use a job description and a time line, and review them with the prospect. This will help give the individual an immediate sense of confidence.

- Show how the assignment fits into the larger development plan and meets your organization's goals. Provide a copy of the case statement, strategic plan, and other written materials that relate to the task.

- Provide specific information on how staff members will provide support. *Solid staff support to help the volunteer succeed is critical.* Provide examples of the kinds of staff help that will be made available.

- If the task involves fundraising, ask for an appropriate gift from the prospective volunteer. He or she cannot be credible with others without having made a financial commitment commensurate with the level of gifts being solicited.

RECOGNIZING AND THANKING VOLUNTEERS

Just as the means of saying a proper "thank you" to donors to your nonprofit is a step toward receiving the next gift, your meaningful expression of appreciation to volunteers serves to cultivate them for continuing or future service. There are also other useful byproducts of the attention you pay to your volunteers, including: 1) the enhancement of your ability to enlist other volunteers; 2) expansion of the visibility of and appreciation for your organization; and 3) garnering more attention to the fundraising programs, the organization's needs, and its ability to attract quality people to serve as volunteers.

Recognition can take many forms and occur in a number of locations. Determining the best is a matter of your knowledge of the individuals and your judgment about what would please them. Do not wed yourself to one or two means of recognition or saying thank you. The typical luncheon or dinner can be very effective in giving public exposure to the volunteers and your organization. However, there are those who would most appreciate receiving their award or gift in a private meeting at their home or office. In all cases, keep these six points in mind when deciding how, where, and when to recognize or thank a volunteer:

1. Does the type of recognition or expression of thanks move the volunteer closer to your organization?

2. Is it appropriate to the task completed by the volunteer?

3. Does it provide an opportunity to build the public image of your organization?

4. Should family members and friends be invited to the recognition event?

5. Will the effort to recognize and thank satisfy the volunteer's need to belong?

6. Ask "How would I react if the organization did this for me?"

Expressing appreciation should be more than a one-time event. People who volunteer have a sense of belonging that is one of the important needs being met. Make certain that each volunteer receives regular personal communications from the CEO and staff member who work with them. These can take the forms of birthday, anniversary, Christmas, and Easter cards, handwritten notes of congratulations on milestones in business, personal deliveries of materials, invitations to special events, and other such human contacts. Individuals normally enjoy receiving plaques, paperweights, etc., but they value more the honest expressions of appreciation that are ongoing in nature.

DEALING WITH RECALCITRANCE

The best efforts you have made in identifying, recruiting, and training a volunteer can never account for difficulties that arise with some who are not following through on the tasks they agreed to do. When this happens, the volunteer must be dealt with in a caring, understanding way that will continue a good relationship with your nonprofit while not adversely affecting other volunteers on the team. We suggest the following in dealing with these individuals understanding that, in each case, the reasons for the unwanted behavior will be different from person to person.

- First, check to make certain that everything promised to the volunteer has been done. You do not want to be embarrassed because the individual was not given the promised support.

- Reacquaint yourself with the process used to recruit the volunteer and the conditions under which he or she agreed to help. Sometimes, individuals are in groupings where they feel pressure to make commitments with which they are later uncomfortable.

- Make an appointment with the volunteer in a setting where the individual will be at ease. This could be a breakfast, lunch, or a meeting in the volunteer's home or office.

- At the meeting, review the progress overall that is being made. Note that some of the volunteer's assignments have not yet been done, and ask if more or different kinds of help are needed. It is often necessary to ask if something has changed in their business or personal lives that make accomplishing the tasks more difficult. Try to have a frank discussion about the barriers to the volunteer's success and be ready to offer to relieve the individual of the responsibility. Do this with a full measure of understanding and caring, being certain to express appreciation for the individual's commitment to your organization.

Directly confronting volunteers in the manner suggested may seem harsh, but it is our experience that gains are made through these sessions, and stronger bonds are created with you and your nonprofit. You and the recalcitrant volunteer will have built a better relationship, and you will have learned what the strengths of the individual are that can be put to use in the future.

In Summary

Most organizations have too few, rather than too many, opportunities for appropriate involvement of volunteers. The answer to achieving success lies in broadening the ownership of your organization's mission and needs beyond the "inside group" to include those who have the means to accomplish your goals and objectives. The right volunteers properly informed, recruited, and trained are an essential part of your development team. Make certain, though, that you have sufficient staff and time to serve the volunteer committees and teams that you have established. Volunteers can be as needy as they are useful. Finally, do not let "bad apples" continue to ferment. They will have a deleterious impact on other volunteers and need to be dealt with in an expeditious and kind manner. Remember, the bottom line is that everything we do in development should be building—not destroying—relationships with everyone who is involved with our nonprofits.

CHAPTER 9

Building and Keeping an Effective Governing Board

Whom are we being led to admire today? Whom should we hold as examples that inspire us to lives that are enriching to ourselves and others? Who will keep our nonprofits healthy, growing, and able to serve societal needs?

In our modern world, identifying role models and heroes can be both confusing and frustrating because we are pointed in the wrong directions. We are often encouraged through media and others to emulate persons of celebrity whose talents as performers are usually better than the examples they set through their behaviors. We are taught in some of our schools that those historical figures whom we thought were great men and women had imperfections that diminish their otherwise heroic accomplishments. We are misled to focus on the flaws rather than the accomplishments that have—and are—giving us the solid platform to build our own lives of purpose.

Heroes and good role models live and work among us whether or not they receive the accolades they deserve. Some are easier to identify when we take the time to notice. These are the firefighters, police officers, emergency medical technicians, and others who respond with courage when summoned, the bravery and dedication of our servicemen and women, and the responders to the victims of the disasters produced by hurricanes and earthquakes.

Less easy to identify are the positive role models who do not make headlines fighting our country's enemies and rescuing people from distress. These are the quiet heroes who serve our vital nonprofit organizations. They would never identify themselves as special, but they devote a significant part of their time, talent, and treasure to improving the condition of their fellow human beings. These heroes serve as members of boards of directors of our nation's colleges, universities, health care institutions, social service agencies, religious organizations, museums, symphonies, foundations, and youth organizations. They provide their time, their leadership, their knowledge, their skills, their wisdom, and their financial resources to guarantee that those institutions we value—and are vital to preserve our American republic—continue to serve all of us. They are the kind of everyday heroes that President Bush (41) began recognizing in the "Thousand Points of Light" Awards and that are now given by the Foundation of the same name.

Let us remember, as discussed previously, that this pervasive volunteer leadership in our society is uniquely American. Largely because we have tended to rely on ourselves and our neighbors instead of government, we have preserved and nurtured a way of life that is both enabling and caring.

You may have decided by now that we have presented an idealized view of those who serve on nonprofit boards. You may also be concerned about the level of commitment and service your organization is receiving from members of your board. This may not be the fault of anyone in particular, but the result of the methods used in selecting board members. Experiences have taught us that a principal problem is that the chief executives and board members are often not "in sync" because neither have an understanding of the others' expectations. This is typically the outcome of the manner by which board members were selected and recruited. The following is a true, but far too common story of the board member recruitment process.

> Without benefit of an active nominating committee (though the committee exists in the structure), the board chair and the executive director have a telephone conference regarding some individuals whom they think would be good board members. "Good" is often a synonym for "having lots of money" and is especially true in this case. The fact that none of these people have close ties with the organization nor have demonstrated any real interest in its work does not appear to be important. The board chair believes that at least two of them "owe" him a favor, and he is certain that he can convince them to serve. He volunteers to call them that very week. The executive director is pleased because the board meeting is the following week, and she must propose two names to fill vacancies created by a like number who could not succeed themselves.
>
> True to his word, the board chair calls the prospective board members—both of whom offer a number of valid reasons for saying "no." To overcome their objections, the board chair tells them that the organization really just needs their names; that they needn't feel obligated to come to every meeting, and they won't have to do very much. The topic of giving money does not come up. Both ultimately agree and are elected by the board on the recommendation of the "nominating committee," the executive director, and the board chair. Less than a year later, the executive director is disappointed because

these members are not active nor have they responded to invitations to support the annual fund.

This story may be too extreme an example to apply to your organization, but some elements of it may have struck home. In any case, it is always helpful to review the process you are using to determine if your board member selection, cultivation, and recruitment strategies could be made more productive. This chapter will discuss the steps to take in preparing to build a strong and effective board, and will deal with the process of cultivating, recruiting, and maintaining the board your organization needs to be successful.

THE PRINCIPAL FUNCTIONS OF THE BOARD

> The wealth needed from the trustees is not only financial wealth, but also wealth in spirit. The loyal trustee is not only asked to dig deep into his or her financial resources, but also to consider the effect of his or her contribution. A contribution has power far beyond its intrinsic worth. Its timing and size (and sometimes its matching conditions) can be an important inspiration to others, but more importantly, when the gift is given in the proper spirit, a thoughtful or handsome contribution is a joy to both the giver and the entire receiving community.
>
> —HENRY D. SHARPE, JR.,
> VICE CHANCELLOR, BROWN UNIVERSITY
> AND CAMPAIGN CHAIR,
> THE CAMPAIGN FOR BROWN, 1979–84

Fair or not, the common perception of board members is that they are only chosen for their ability to make large gifts and to get similar gifts from their friends. While it is important that every board member give to the organization they own, effective boards should be built with an understanding of what the nonprofit needs to accomplish its mission. Wealth is not the only—nor the most important—quality needed in every board member.

There are four primary responsibilities of board members—individually and collectively—that we first learned in the 1980's from our consultant, Robert Stuhr.

1. **Policymaker**—To ensure that the mission of the organization is accurate and that the organization's plans and programs are within the scope of the mission. To be able to make informed decisions, each board member should: 1) know a great deal about the organization; 2) keep informed about trends in the field and what is happening at other organizations with similar missions; and 3) be aware of the changes in society that may make an impact on their organization's programs and services.

2. **Steward**—To insist on sound business management principles and practices to protect the funds and properties of the organization. This means that the board must take care to adopt a budget that enables the organization to operate programs and services consistent with the mission. In the case of nonprofits that have endowments, good stewardship includes guidance and review of the investment policies and management of invested resources.

3. **Ambassador**—To interpret the organization and its programs of service to prospective donors and the larger community. Directors should: 1) expect to be kept informed; 2) tell the story of the organization at every appropriate opportunity; 3) look for occasions to speak or invite others to speak about the organization in their churches and clubs; 4) advise the CEO and other board members about rumors and help correct erroneous perceptions; and 5) assist individuals with whom they have influence to learn about the mission and work of the organization.

4. **Builder**—To be responsible for building and sustaining a comprehensive development program, ensuring the long-term ability of the organization to fund its programs and fulfill its mission. Effective board members make certain that their organization: 1) provides leadership in creating and updating a strategic plan that gives the organization its specific direction; 2) provides for financial stability and growth by building an annual fund program for current operations as well as an ongoing program for raising major gifts during lifetime or through estate planning; 3) helps to involve many volunteers, not only in raising funds, but also in strengthening the organization's public perception and brand; 4) provides information to develop the best strategies to engage others in the support of the organization; 5) makes an annual gift to the organization commensurate with ability; 6) makes an appropriate capital gift either during lifetime or through estate planning; and 7) assists in identifying, cultivating, and, if appropriate, soliciting gifts.

You may have often heard candidates for and members of boards (yours included) who profess not to want to ask people for money. Not every board member should be required to directly ask for a gift, but EVERY board member should be actively involved in your nonprofit's development program. There are many intentional ways that a member can tell the story of your organization through arranging speaking engagements for the executive director and others at their clubs, hosting a breakfast, lunch, dinner, or cocktail reception on behalf of your nonprofit to enable the invitees to learn about your organization, helping to set up one-on-one appointments with business and personal friends with representatives of your organization, and, of course, providing names and information on prospective major donors. All of these are short of actually asking for a gift, but they are essential to making a successful ask possible. Learn the comfort levels of each board member and utilize them within their comfort zone. Remember, they want to be a successful board member as much as you want them to be.

BEGINNING TO BUILD A STRONG BOARD

> A strong board of trustees does not guarantee a strong institution, but every strong institution has a strong board of trustees. Where boards have been strong, well organized and committed, the institutions, while they may be undergoing financial pressure, still face the future with expectations of success and continued viability. Where the board is weak, badly organized, and un-committed (often non-committed) the institution is usually in deep trouble.
>
> —ARLO SCHILLING, FORMER PRESIDENT,
> NORTH CENTRAL COLLEGE

The poet and wit Ogden Nash in his "Ode to Duty" reflected the feelings of most of us who know what we ought to do—what we have agreed to do—but just do not want to do it.

> O Duty!
> Why hast thou not the visage
> of a sweetie or a cutie?
> Thou so ubiquitous,
> And I so iniquitous.

Whenever we feel we have been pressured by employer/spouse/friends to do some task that does not really interest us; whenever guilt is the motivating force; whenever we are repaying a "favor"; whenever . . . well, you can finish the list, we approach the task with a leaden spirit. We feel the weight of doing our duty when the task does not meet our needs nor our self-confidence that we can achieve it.

How differently we feel when the performance of any task meets one or more needs within us. Then, the job, no matter how onerous it may be to someone else, is not a "duty," but a fulfilling experience. That is why some people can work with joy in a daycare center with infants who need special care, changing diapers, wiping small noses, rocking babies to sleep. Others who find this distasteful may serve the same agency by giving money and helping lead others to support the program. When volunteers are engaged in activities in which they feel comfort and have strengths, it is not a duty, but provides satisfaction.

What we own we value, whether it be physical property or volunteers activity. At the board level, this rather basic principle is not always applied. Our zeal to get Mr. or Ms. Deep Pockets sometimes causes us to shorten the process of research, cultivation, and involvement before the invitation to board membership is extended. Strong boards are filled with those who have ownership of the organization and their particular roles as board members.

There are several factors that will enable the process of building a strong and effective board for your organization.

- Productive board building can only begin if the board leadership and the CEO are ready. This cannot be forced on the board, but it must come from the members' understanding and acceptance that a more beneficial process must be put in place.

- The mission of the organization must be clear and current and understood by current board members.

- The leadership of the board must be involved in creating, reviewing, and recommending the procedures for evaluating current board members and the selection of potential board members.

- The board must be clear and united about what it expects of its members. This means that there is a job description that has been reviewed and adopted by the board that clearly specifies their roles and responsibilities.

- There is agreement on the kind of board that is needed, including the skills, knowledge, market segments, and professions of future board members.

- There is a formal process for nominations to be made and managed. Nomination forms are distributed for the use of board members, and no one is considered for membership without the submitted form.

- There is a written plan of action to reach board-generated goals. A written plan with measurable goals will help make certain that there will be efforts made to achieve them.

- The board is organized—with the proper committee structures—to oversee and provide leadership to the organization.

None of the above can be imposed on board members but must come through a process of self-examination and planning. We suggest—and rather strongly—that every board should meet annually, to focus on itself, and to assess and set objectives for board health and growth for the succeeding year. Even as brief a time as a two-hour session properly facilitated can help your board see itself more clearly, identify strengths and weaknesses, and agree upon the specific tasks that the board will work to accomplish during the next twelve months.

For boards to be strong and effective, the members must own their board as much or more than they own the organization.

CREATING AND GUIDING THE PROCESS—THE "COMMITTEE ON BOARD WELLNESS"

The most important committee of the board—and most often neglected—is the one that has the ongoing responsibility for board health, strength, and membership. It is known by many names—Nominating Committee, Committee on Board Affairs, Board Development Committee—but more accurately should be thought of as the "Committee on Board Wellness." When properly organized and seriously operating, this committee can and should be the driving force in building and maintaining a productive, strong board that enables the organization to fulfill its mission of service.

The committee's responsibilities begin with the current board, helping fellow members fully to understand and appreciate their significant leadership roles. The work of the committee includes:

- Analyzing the current board make-up and creating for board approval a profile of future members
- Creating, evaluating, and managing a pool of potential candidates for board membership
- Guiding the process of cultivating prospective board members
- Drafting a board job description and/or conducting an annual review of the document, recommending any necessary changes in language, board structure, etc.
- Nominating prospective board members and preparing the slate of officers for the board
- Assisting the chair of the board in making committee assignments
- Conducting periodic evaluations of members of the board within meetings of the committee and by board members themselves
- Working with the chair of the board and the CEO in planning and facilitating member orientation and continuing education

Considerations in Selecting Board Members

Organizations are different in their missions, purposes, and personalities. Therefore, no two boards will be the same, though there are some similar traits that every board should have. The following are internal and external considerations in selecting potential board members.

- Internal
  - What kind of organization are you—local, regional, national?
  - What goals must you accomplish to fulfill your mission?
  - What is the current make-up of your board—professions and affiliations?
  - Which of your target markets are represented and where is representation needed?
  - What does the CEO expect?
  - Do you have a religious affiliation?
  - What size board do you need to achieve your goals?
  - What is the personality and character of your current board?
- External
  - What is the makeup of your constituency?
  - What is the current visibility and perception of your organization?
  - What are the levels and spheres of influence of potential board candidates in your target markets—professional/business standing and/or philanthropic leadership?

There are also attributes that are desirable in all potential board members. The most notable are Walter B. Wriston's three W's—Work, Wealth, and Wisdom. Some wag simplified the qualifications to "give, get, or get off," though this does not incorporate other important qualities needed in a board that will be able properly to own and serve your organization. We have added DeWitt's Five I's—Integrity, Intelligence, Intuitiveness, Industry, and Influence. One absolute requirement, however, is that the proposed board member will have demonstrated his or her understanding of and commitment to the mission of your organization. Those who are primarily interested in enhancing their resumes will not likely be very helpful to your nonprofit.

Board member slots are few, so that each person under consideration should have the ability to move the organization toward its goals in one or more ways. (See the discussion of the Move Management program in Chapter 6.) For some, this may be entré to individuals of wealth or access to market segments not previously available. For others, it may be depth of professional knowledge that will measurably improve your financial management, organizational methods, and public profile. Still, others may give insight into the clients your nonprofit is serving to make certain that assumptions are replaced with facts.

All members of your board should possess integrity and credibility. That goes without saying, you say to yourself. Of course, your CEO and board members expect that in themselves and those who are invited to become members. However, it does need to be clearly stated so that these qualities are always in the forefront of your consideration of anyone to join the select group that is your board.

Some Concerns to Keep in Mind

As you learn more about board member candidates through research and the cultivation process, there are a few warning signs to be aware of. Take note of the candidates:

- **Educational level**—will he/she feel comfortable with the other board members? We know of good people who have felt intimidated because they did not possess the schooling and degrees of the majority of the board. Usually, this can be resolved at the point of recruitment by making certain the board members know exactly why they have been asked to serve.

- **Attitude about wealth**—will he/she use it to influence the board? Some individuals who are significantly wealthier and influential than the other board members will attempt to unduly influence decisions. It is difficult for the less well-off members to counter such a person, and decisions that fundamentally change your organization can be made that are not in the best interests of the public you serve. As difficult as it may be to deny the individual a seat at the table, the board must have the courage to say "no."

- **Religious faith**—or lack of it. This can have a profound impact on your organization depending on your mission and your affiliations. The intentions and the culture of your board and nonprofit can be positively or negatively affected by the wrong choice.

- **Team player**—How will she/he work and play with others? Every board member should bring one or more strengths to the organization and be free to give advice and express opinions. However, each board member should also give and receive respect for the board to function productively.

The Invitation Sets the Tone

How a prospective board member is invited to join the board will largely determine whether or not the individual and your organization will have a successful partnership. Remembering the example earlier in this chapter, too often board members are inadequately prepared and too carelessly asked to accept membership in the most important club of your organization. Therefore, once a prospective member has been sufficiently researched, cultivated, and involved, the invitation should be extended in a serious and purposeful manner.

First, the candidate's name should have been brought to the board by the committee responsible for managing nominations. After the presentation of the candidate and any questions have been answered, the full board should vote to accept the individual for membership. No invitation should be extended to anyone without prior approval by the board.

Following this step, an appointment should be made by the CEO and/or the board member who will be a participant in the meeting. This should always be a face-to-face meeting, not a telephone call.

Prepare for the meeting by creating a packet of materials to share with the prospective board member. The materials assembled should include an executive summary of the latest audit and current financial statement, board job description, board organizational chart, a listing of board goals and progress toward them, a list of current board members and their affiliations, the executive summary of the current strategic plan, an executive summary of the internal case statement, and a description of annual and major giving objectives.

The discussion should include an explanation of how and why he or she was nominated and approved by the board for membership. In particular, the candidate should be given a specific explanation of the particular strengths he or she would bring to the board and the organization. This makes certain that the individual is clear that the choice made was a thoughtful one, and lends more seriousness to the invitation.

The candidate also should be made aware of the challenges the organization faces or will be facing. These may include achieving sufficient annual support or capital goals, accreditations, staffing, and program issues. Be forthcoming about everything that will make an impact on the nonprofit with which the board must deal. Furthermore, all questions—whether or not they are uncomfortable—must be answered honestly and fully.

Finally, do not assume the prospective board member will understand the requirement to make an annual and/or capital gift commensurate with ability to do so. We do not advocate a minimum annual gift to become a board member; however, it must be clear from the outset that 100% participation in giving is an expectation.

As with most invitations will demand significant commitment of time, talent, and resources, the candidate will very likely want time to think it over. Ask how much time and if there are additional pieces of information that will enable a full consideration of the request. It is best to get agreement on a date and time when the decision will be made, and the method of contact.

No one can predict with absolute certainty that by following these steps you will acquire a fully involved and productive board member. But, you will certainly increase the likelihood that it will be the case. A thorough, systematic, open approach in this process—from start to finish—will help you build the board your organization needs to be successful.

The CEO and The Board—Who's in Charge Here?

A college board chair whom a friend encountered some years ago would begin each board meeting with the same agenda item: Shall we fire the president today? To his credit, he did not mean this to be a jest. This was his way of forcing the board to think about their support of the CEO they had hired and in whom they had placed chief management responsibility. If they did not feel confidence in the president, then it would have a detrimental effect upon them and the entire school.

Before he became president of Bridgewater College in Virginia, trustee Phillip Stone said this in an address to development professionals and nonprofit CEOs:

> Trustees should recognize and accept their legal prerogative to act as owners or owner's representatives in serving as board members. When trustees fully understand this responsibility, they will be much more conscientious and sensitive about their fiduciary obligation to be accountable for the performance of the institution and its improvement. A person who attends a board meeting on a monthly, quarterly, or less frequent basis and does not feel a sense of accountability, may see it as not more than a social activity. Some trustees, to their regret, learn through legal proceedings that they have substantial fiduciary, legal, and financial responsibilities for the organization. It is tempting to believe that recommendations can be approved merely because they come from the administration so that no significant board analysis is needed. From the mindset of being an owner and accountable to a constituency, board members are likely to ask better questions and to require more information.

As a matter of efficient use of time and expertise, it is a prudent practice for board members to hire the best senior management person possible and give him or her the authority necessary to administer the organization. It would be counterproductive for board members individually to attempt to do the job the board has chosen to delegate to the CEO. Once that important decision has been made—and board members do not want to fire the president today—then the executive deserves the support of the board in the decisions that he or she must make within the policy guidelines the board has adopted.

An analogy from the world of sports may underscore the important, but separate, roles played by the owner (the board) and the manager/coach (the CEO). When a team owner attempts to interfere or "help" the coach manage the team, even the most talented players never seem to produce championships.

KEEPING IT IN THE FAMILY—THOUGHTS ON BOARD RELATIONS

Board members should never feel reluctant to tackle tough issues—even with fellow members—but the discussion should be kept within proper channels and done at appropriate times. Usually, these discussions can be held with the organization's leadership outside of the formal board meeting. However, sometimes, it must be done within the board meeting itself. When this happens, the aim should be to make certain all of the facts are known and that the best decisions are made—not to embarrass a fellow member.

Vigorous discussion in board meetings can be healthy exercises *as long as the board faces the public united.* A board acts as a unit—no single board member is authorized to act independently, except to the extent permitted by the bylaws and board policy. Your constituency should never know that the board had a tough debate on anything. Once the decision is made, support it. If a board member cannot in good conscience back the particular decision or action, then he or she must resign. Airing any dirty laundry does no benefit to the organization, nor to the person spreading information inappropriately.

Strong boards are composed of people whose first concern is the organization's agenda, and leave personal agendas outside the board room. The CEO bears considerable responsibility for building and keeping productive relationships with the board and the organization. Board members need to be seen or called between meetings by the CEO to give them updates and ask their input. This provides opportunities, as well, for continual assessments of whether board members are being used effectively and to their best advantage. Building and keeping a strong board requires continual attention throughout the year, so that your organization becomes and remains a high priority for each of them.

THE SPECIAL CHARACTER OF FOUNDATION BOARDS

We have spent this chapter discussing typical governing boards that have multifaceted roles in providing the proper levels of oversight, funding, and promoting the organizations they own. There is another kind of nonprofit whose board has a more precise task—that of raising and distributing funds to other nonprofit organizations. Included in the members' job description are the typical financial management and ambassadorial functions. However, their main responsibility is raising funds. They are, in fact, akin to the development and marketing standing committee of a traditional board, and each of their members must understand and accept his or her role in fundraising.

Most of these types of nonprofits were established to raise money for particular organizations—hospitals, retirement communities and nursing facilities, membership groups. In the case of healthcare facilities, foundations were born at a time when the federal laws concerning Medicaid did not permit the organizations to raise money to offset the extra costs. Though that law no longer applies, these foundations have continued to raise support for their parent organization. In the case of membership groups—501(c)(2) organizations—related foundations enable fundraising for projects and services that support and promote the particular interests of the trade or professional association.

An example of the latter is the I-CAR Educational Foundation that was set up by I-CAR, a membership organization whose purpose is to keep collision repair technicians up-to-date on the newest automobile body construction, finishes, etc. and to provide the necessary training. This is done mostly by volunteers in state committees. The leadership of I-CAR decided that it could benefit the collision repair industry by creating a state-of-the art curriculum for vocational schools and encouraging young people to consider the field as a vocational option. Because this undertaking would require a considerable amount of money, it was decided to establish a 501(c)(3) foundation with its own board and staff to raise the funds for the curriculum and determine other long-term projects that would benefit the vocation and, ultimately, the driving public. This Foundation was successfully created with a minimal staff and strong board that raised the initial funding for the curriculum, and has continued to serve the educational needs of the collision repair industry.

As with all boards whose primary purpose is giving and influencing others to give, those identified for membership are often individuals of greater wealth and corporate status than the members of the parent organization board. This fact does not mean that one board is inferior to the other; it is merely to acknowledge the different roles and, hence, abilities needed in the two boards. Understanding that from the outset will help you design programs and other means to build and maintain good relationships between members of the boards. Here are a few ways to keep the focus on the organization's needs on the part of these boards:

- The executive director of the membership organization should be the CEO of the foundation.
- Several members of the membership organization board should be appointed to the foundation board.
- An annual joint board retreat for planning and team building should be considered.
- Strategic planning for the membership organization should also include the foundation board members.

- Each board should regularly report to the other on its work and priorities.
- Make certain the foundation board understands that decisions and priorities that affect the parent organization can only be made by the organization's board.

IN SUMMARY

Being a member of a board has been defined as the holding of a charter of public trust for an organization. In the past, trustees have been respected as owners who guarded, protected, and conserved their organizations. Board members have been expected to hold the line, to observe traditions, to react wisely and cautiously, to be a court of last resort. However, boards can no longer see their roles as preservationists. Such a view will eventually put themselves and their organizations out of business.

There is still a need for the traditional role of board members. But, an important new dimension must be added—a positive, active role. No longer can board members just react to what is put before them. They must initiate. No longer can they simply hold the public trust. Their jobs now require that they take leadership in generating trust and, thereby, strengthening the work of others in their organizations in building trust within their constituency and society.

Character does matter. Board members are needed who are willing to exemplify sound character and will work to insure that their nonprofits maintain unimpeachable standards.

For board members to be willing to invest their own character—their reputations in the leadership of their institutions—it is important that their ownership be deeper than their names on the letterhead and in the annual report. Strong boards are filled with those who understand and own the missions as much or more than they legally own the institutions.

As the late Robert Stuhr used to tell boards he addressed: "It's an honor to be a board member, but the job is not honorary." Strong boards have members who:

- Know and appreciate the organization they serve, and the key role each of them play as board members
- Have a sense of shared responsibility and *esprit de corps*. They help to promote unity even though they may disagree during discussions on particular issues
- Understand the importance of recruiting the best to serve with them and help identify and cultivate those who would be good future board members

- Move forward as partners with the organization's leadership, with a full appreciation of the need to meet the challenges ahead
- Are organized so that each board member can make his or her special contribution to the development of the organization

Finally, a strong board will insist that the organization continue to look to the future—to resist the temptation to be comfortable with the ways things are at the moment. The only constant is change, and it is up to the board to make certain that the CEO work with them in an ongoing review of programs, funding, staffing, and, most important, mission. Perhaps, the single most important question that board and staff leadership should continually ask is "what if . . . ?" Strategic visioning and planning should have a permanent place in the organizational structure of your board, and in the fiber of its members. It is through ongoing evaluation and planning that your organization will keep its mission current and its services relevant to society.

SUGGESTED JOB DESCRIPTION	PRONINO USA BOARD OF DIRECTORS JOB DESCRIPTION

Responsibilities of the Board of Directors[1]

I. Governance and Policy Creation
   a. Establish, articulate, and promote the mission and vision of PNUSA.
   b. Ensure that PNUSA policies, procedures, and practices are in compliance with federal and state law, relevant agency regulation, the Articles of Incorporation and the Bylaws of PNUSA.
   c. Establish and oversee committees of the Board of Directors. Develop broad policies to guide PNUSA.
   d. In all of its activities, the authority of the Board of Directors rest in the Board as a whole and not in its individual members.

II. Stewardship
   a. Act as fiduciary and guardian of all PNUSA assets.
   b. Develop and approve the budget.
   c. Review and analyze financial reports to determine effectiveness of expenditures to meet the mission of PNSUA and make recommendations for improvements.
   d. Develop and approve financial planning and investments.
   e. Ensure the highest level of financial accountability and transparency through the development of policies and procedures that reflect best practices for nonprofit management.

---

[1] Adapted and used with permission from ProNino USA

f. Honor the good will of donors by ensuring that PNUSA resources are utilized to achieve the charitable aims of PNUSA in an effective and efficient manner.

III. Builder
   a. Board
      i. Take leadership in strategic planning both in the creation and implementation of the strategic objectives.
      ii. Provide for self-sustainability through identification, cultivation, and education of new Board members.
      iii. Conduct regular self-assessment and education activities.
      iv. Evaluate the performances of the Board officers and committee chairs.
   b. Financial Resources
      i. Secure the resources necessary to fund the mission of PNUSA.
      ii. Establish fundraising goals and objectives.
      iii. Provide planning and oversight for the achievement of these goals.
      iv. Participate as appropriate in raising the annual operating and capital funds needed by PNUSA.

IV. Ambassador
   a. Promote and protect the image of PNUSA.
   b. Serve as a respected representative of the organization.
   c. Seek out opportunities to tell others about the mission, vision, and work of PNUSA.
   d. Help to productively involve others in the work of PNUSA.

V. Operational Leadership
   a. Recruit, hire, evaluate and, if deemed necessary, replace the chief executive officer and top management.
   b. Establish and regularly evaluate executive compensation.
   c. Identify and/or develop programs and partnerships that fulfill the mission of PNUSA.
   d. Establish and oversee policies, procedures, and agreements with partners and program leaders that enable PNUSA to maintain the highest level of transparency, accountability, and effectiveness in fulfilling its mission.
   e. Serve as the final court of appeals for staff members and other groups or individuals who disagree with decisions of the administration

Responsibilities of Individual Members of the Board

I. Each member of the Board of Directors shall:
   a. Serve PNUSA to the best of his or her ability by giving ample time, care, and consideration in the performance of his or her duties as Director.
   b. Accept the responsibilities described above ("Responsibilities of the Board of Directors") and will actively participate in fulfilling these duties.

    c. Act and make decisions that are in the best interests of PNUSA without consideration of personal, business or private interest. Each Director shall follow PNUSA's Conflict of Interest Policy.

    d. Ensure that important issues are brought to the Board, be willing to challenge other's positions, vote according to his/her conscious and be willing to work with fellow board members in a spirit of cooperation

    e. Maintain the confidential nature of Board deliberations

    f. Serve on at least one committee.

    g. Familiarize him/herself with the programs and operations of PNUSA and, as able, will participate in on-site program evaluations to gain greater understanding of the work of PNUSA.

    h. Participate in the fundraising efforts of PNUSA, including regular, personal financial contributions made in accordance with the individual ability.

    i. Identify and cultivate potential donors and new Board of Directors members within his or her sphere of influence and in the wider community. A director wil. provide suggestions for the development of new sources of income and/or Board of Directors members for the organization

    j. Serve as ambassador for PNUSA, seeking to protect, preserve, and promote the image and work of PNUSA.

II. Each Director will be provided regular financial and other reports relating to the health and status of PNUSA.

III. Each Director can expect prompt and thorough answers to questions as needed to fulfill his or her legal, fiduciary, and moral obligations to PNUSA.

Committees of the Board of Directors

In order to better perform its duties and fulfill its mission, PNUSA has established the following committees that are governed by the Policy on Committee Formation and Function:

I. The Executive Committee acts for the Board during the period between Board meetings, and is elected by the Board. The actions of the Executive Committee are subject to ratification by the entire Board. The Executive Committee shall ensure that PNUSA's policies, procedures, and practices are in compliance with all federal, state, and local laws and regulations as well as the Articles of Incorporation, and Bylaws of PNUSA. This committee is responsible for overseeing and coordinating the development of broad policies to guide the organization in it operations.

II. The Committee on Board Affairs investigates and proposes prospective Directors, nominates officers of the Board, and often assists the chair of the Board on making committee assignments.

    a. The Committee analyzes the kinds of talents needed on the Board and its committees.

    b. The Committee must note and follow the Board's policy in rotation.

    c. This committee shall have the responsibility of reviewing Director performance as well as working with the chairs of the Board and President/Executive Director of the organization in planning Director

III. Committee on Programs has the responsibility for establishing broad policies and a program of review in the following areas:

    a. Current programs—Develop, negotiate and oversee agreements with Partner Organizations and Affiliates that ensure that funds expended achieve program goals and further the mission of PNUSA. Establish and cultivate relationships with Partners Organizations and Affiliates to ensure open and clear communication regarding the operation of programs. Secure adequate financial and program reports from Partners and Affiliates.

    b. Program planning

      i. Identify and/or develop programs and partnerships that further the mission of PNUSA.

      ii. Research and compare similar programs to determine relative effectiveness and incorporate changes to improve programs.

IV. The Committee on Finance and Investments has the responsibility for establishing broad policies and a program for review in the following areas:

    a. Long-range financial planning

    b. Investments

    c. Budget

    d. Records and systems

    e. Audit

    f. Supervision of all real estate and all auxiliary enterprises

V. Committee on Development and Public Relations has the responsibility for establishing basic policies and a program of review in the following areas:

    a. Publicity, publications, public relations, and special events which will enhance the prestige of the organization

    b. Fundraising programs which will seek gifts from individuals, Trustee/Directors, firms, foundations, and churches, for the purpose of

      i. The Annual Fund for support of current operations

      ii. Projects in the strategic long-range plan

      iii. Capital fund programs (endowment and facilities

      iv. Planned giving (wills and bequests, life income contracts, insurance, trusts, etc.)

      v. Special events

      vi. The Development and Public Relations Committee plans and recommends programs through which all Trustee/Directors can fulfill their development responsibilities.

VI. The Board of Directors may establish other standing and ad hoc committees as necessary and appropriate.

SAMPLE BOARD MEMBER NOMINATION FORM

To: Committee on Board Affairs

I wish to recommend the following person to be considered as a member of the Board of Directors of (institution):

Name: _____

Address: _____

_____

Reason for my recommendation: _____

_____
_____
_____
_____
_____
_____
_____
_____

Signed_____

Date: _____

Confidential Nominee Information

1. Name: _____ Telephone: (H) _____
   Address: _____
   Email: _____
   Phone (H): _____
   Phone (O): _____
   Cell: _____
   Information: _____
   Spouse: _____
   Colleges/Degrees: _____
   Children: _____
   Other training: _____
   Financial information: _____
   Other: _____
   _____

2. Interests, volunteer activities, board memberships, civic clubs, etc.:
   _____

3. Involvement with (organization): _____

4. Strength(s) nominee brings to the board: _____

5. Contributions (to be provided by development office): _____
   _____
   _____
   _____

BOARD MEMBER BIOGRAPHICAL INFORMATION

Name: _____   Date: _____

Occupation: _____

Home Address: _____   Home Phone ( ) _____

   Cell Phone ( ) _____

   Home Fax ( ) _____

Business _____   Bus. Phone ( ) _____

   Bus. Fax ( ) _____

Email: _____

Birthday: _____

Name of Spouse: _____   Birthday: _____

Spouse's Occupation: _____   Anniversary: _____

Children

Name: _____

School(s), recognitions, etc. _____

Name: _____   Age: _____

School(s), recognitions, etc. _____

Name: _____   Age: _____

School(s), recognitions, etc. _____

Education:

High school: _____ Graduation date: _____

Colleges, dates attended, degrees: _____

College recognitions/honors: _____

Business or professional responsibilities and titles: _____

Corporate boards/officers: _____

Civic clubs/offices: _____

Social/service clubs and offices: _____

Church/synagogue/mosque membership: _____

Nonprofit board memberships (including foundations) and offices: _____

_____

_____

Honors/recognitions: _____

Publications/speeches: _____

Hobbies: _____

Other philanthropic interests: _____

Additional comments/information: _____

BOARD MEMBER SELF EVALUATION

The following are areas of Board make up, service, commitment, and effectiveness. Please consider each and rate both your performance and that of the Board.

Please place a check mark in the appropriate box for your answer. When you are finished with this side please complete the sections located on the back of this form.

	Poor	Average	Good	Excellent
Mission and Role				
The Board reviews the mission statement annually to make certain it is current and compelling				
The Board understands the mission and keeps it in mind when reviewing and setting policies				
The Board understands and has reached consensus on the kind of organization it wants				
The Board has among its members the expertise needed to provide oversight of its budget and programs				
The Board reviews and makes policy decisions fairly and objectively				
The Board gives the CEO the necessary authority to run the organization				
The Board has set policies and procedures to ensure sound fiscal management				
The Board takes leadership in strategic planning and implementation				
Board Organization and Development				
New members of the Board receive prompt and complete orientation				
Each new member has a clear understanding of their role				
The Board job description is up-to-date and accurately reflects the members' expectations				
The Board is made up of members with talents and knowledge needed to serve the organization				
The Board is organized to make use of the talents and knowledge of its members				
The frequency and number of meetings enable the Board to perform its work well				
The Board has the right number of members				

	Poor	Average	Good	Excellent
The length of term is right for our Board				
The Board has an effective means to identify, cultivate, and recruit new members				
The Board has the diversity it needs to be effective and credible				
Marketing and Fundraising				
Board members understand their role in marketing/communications and fundraising				
Board members are advocates of the organization and active in telling its story				
Board members actively help raise funds through providing prospects names to soliciting gifts				
Every Board member makes an annual contribution commensurate with ability				
Every Board member has included the organization in their estate plans				
Finances				
The Board carefully considers and approves a budget that enables the organization to accomplish its objectives				
The Board has procedures to provide for careful oversight of the budget				
The Board oversees investment policies to ensure they meet organizational needs				

Comments

What about your service on the Board is most satisfying to you?

_____

_____

_____

What would you like to see changed in the way the Board is structured and operates?

_____

_____

_____

Other comments and suggestions?

_____

_____

_____

BOARD PROFILE WORKSHEET

This worksheet helps to identify current gaps and desired characteristics on our board. The grid is marked for each characteristic that is filled presently by one or more board members. Each NUMBER represents the name of a current board member. Each LETTER represents the name of a prospective board member.

Categories to Consider, if Relevant	Current Board Members												Prospective Board Members										
Area of Interest	1	2	3	4	5	6	7	8	9	10	11	12	A	B	C	D	E	F	G	H	I	J	K
Expertise/Professional Skills, Such As:																							
Organization and Financial Management																							
Health Care Management																							
Administration																							
Business/Corporate Management																							
Finance:																							
Accounting																							
Banking & Trusts																							
Investments																							
Fundraising (experience in raising funds)																							
Law																							
Marketing																							
Strategic Planning																							
Public Relations																							
Real Estate																							
Representatives of Patients/Clients Served																							
Educational Professional																							
Other Skills																							
Age:																							
Under 35																							
35–50																							
51–65																							
Over 65																							

(continued)

(CONTINUED)

Categories to Consider, if Relevant	Current Board Members	Prospective Board Members
Sex:		
Women		
Men		
Race/Ethnic Background:		
African-American		
Hispanic/Latino		
Caucasian		
Other		
Geographical Location:		
Local City		
County		
Region		
State		
Financial Position:		
Self-Employed		
Salaried/Commissioned		
Record of Philanthropy:		
Board Committees		
Board Affairs/Nominating		
Development and PR		
Program:		
Building and Grounds		
Finance and Investments		
Other		
Length of Board Service:		
Over 10 years		
5–10 Years		
2–5 Years		
Less than 2 years		

BOARD OF DIRECTORS DEVELOPMENT AND PUBLIC RELATIONS COMMITTEE

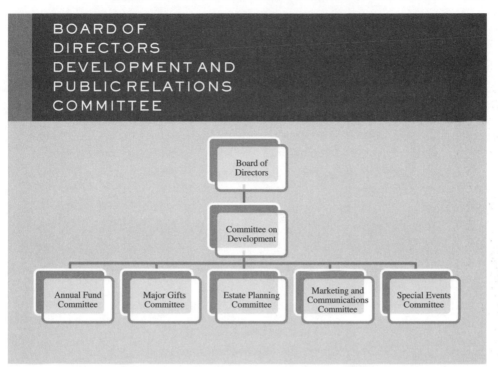

BOARD OF DIRECTORS TYPICAL ORGANIZATION CHART

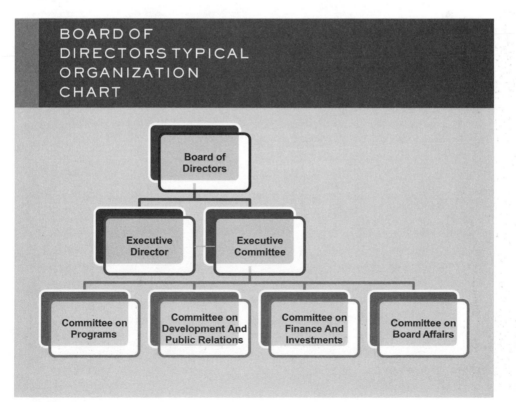

CHAPTER 10

Your Organization's Real Chief Development Officer

"To whom much is given, much is expected." This timeless truism could be applied with vigor to the hope, the trust, and the expectations placed in the chief executives of nonprofit organizations. Many of them must fill multiple roles, especially at small organizations with limited funding. They must be the administrator, public relations director, fundraiser, and spokesperson. Their hours are long, and they are not remunerated sufficiently for their talents and their commitment. But, it is their deep dedication to the mission of their nonprofits and the people they serve that keep most of them engaged for many productive years.

Chief executives of nonprofits are the public embodiment of the mission, the vision, and the public personae of the organizations they lead. The successful ones understand and accept this fact without hubris. They know that productive results for the total development program depend upon the CEO's ability to exemplify the nature, lifestyle, hopes, and aspirations of all those who comprise their organizations at any given moment. As chief executives, they stand as examples both to the internal constituencies (faculty, staff, medical staff, etc.) and to the external constituencies, most especially to those who are prospects to become major benefactors. Major donors are becoming more discriminating in their selections of organizations to support. They want to know what it is the organization is trying to accomplish, and how it expects to achieve its objectives. And, they expect to have their questions answered by the CEO.

As the boards' (the owners') representatives, chief executives have both management and relationship responsibilities to keep their nonprofits running smoothly. They should always strive to keep their board members informed about the state of their organizations, including the financial status, operational needs and difficulties, public relations challenges, and the joys that occur. Their boards carry the fiduciary, legal, and financial responsibilities for their organizations. CEOs should expect board members to ask relevant questions, request additional data, and scrutinize budget and program materials.

The wise CEO cultivates and maintains relationships of mutual trust so that the leadership of the organization faces the internal and external publics united. This means that the CEO should make a priority of contacting each member of the board by telephone, through lunch meetings, and regular communications via e-mail to build good relationships and to learn how the member views his or her board membership. An active outreach will not only prevent problems and avoid strained relationships, but it will help keep board members interested and involved in the organization.

As the real chief development officer, the chief executive must take the lead in communicating the character and goals of the organization. To do this, he or she must learn how constituents currently view the organization, and then provide them with a message that exudes clarity and confidence in the organization's position and direction. If there is development staff to help, the CEO should use this resource in crafting the message and facilitating the exercise of this important responsibility. There is no shame in having drafts of remarks prepared by staff for review and editing by the CEO.

Recognizing that not every nonprofit has even one development officer—let alone a fully staffed development office—a chief executive can be much more effective in discharging this marketing and fundraising responsibility with strong leadership in that role. Most nonprofits do have a director of development; however, the work of the chief executive and the development head will be more productive when these key persons complement each other in administrative skills and working styles. A bond of trust and respect is essential to this relationship for them to be successful in promoting and extending their organization's objectives.

A proper appreciation on the part of the development staff and board members of the central role the chief executive plays in marketing and fundraising is critical, so that all members of the development team can work together in gathering the support the organization needs. However, it is even more important for the chief executive to comprehend his or her importance in raising friends and funds for the organization. Without the CEO's acceptance of this responsibility, the organization will have difficulty attracting the people and resources necessary for it to reach toward its potential.

"TRICKLE DOWN DEVELOPMENT"

As the one ultimately responsible for the organization's success, the chief executive must have a clear understanding of the concept of development and its components. Development does not equal fundraising, though raising money is a part of the process. The effective CEO recognizes that development is a continual effort to foster commitment to the mission and purpose of your organization through building lasting and mutually satisfying relationships with your constituents.

We have previously discussed in some detail the principles of successful development. To review briefly, individuals, corporations, and foundations are attracted to organizations whose mission and objectives resonate with them and meet their needs (marketing). Second, the practice of development does not begin and end in the development office. Every staff member, every board member, every volunteer, and, in some cases, every consumer of your services are integral parts of your ability to engage people and raise money (holistic). Third, development includes fundraising, but only so that you can accomplish those tasks and build facilities that are required to meet your mission.

While the CEO must be concerned about all of the above, it is the "holistic" principle that *only* the chief executive can establish as a priority. What is important to the boss will be important to those who report to him or her and, subsequently, to their subordinates (hence, "trickle down"). Good development questions to ask are: What is the environment at our organization? Are people friendly and helpful? Do visitors feel welcome? Are our students, clients, parents, patients, and consumers treated with respect?

We recommend that staff members be purposely evaluated on their understanding of their responsibilities to create a welcoming organizational environment, and on their performance in carrying the principle out both with your constituencies and fellow staff members. Fostering and institutionalizing a target market attitude is as important as any other aspect of a staff member's work and should be a factor that impacts pay and promotion.

The atmosphere at your organization either enables or frustrates efforts to build the long-term relationships with key prospects necessary to secure their involvement, their ownership of your goals, and their financial support. And, only the chief executive can set the tone and the expectations for an environment that will be productive for your organization.

THE CEO AND THE COMPONENTS OF DEVELOPMENT

The CEO, with the support of the governing board, is responsible for making certain that the organization continues to be relevant, compelling, and has a blueprint for the future. There are some CEOs who have the expressed expectation that the development office head should determine what the fundraising program should address. Of course, the office of development should not determine the goals and objectives of the nonprofit. The development staff serves as managers and facilitators. It is the CEO's responsibility to provide the leadership with the board that will set the organizational vision, priorities, and methods by which these will be communicated within the organization and to the external public.

The CEO's leadership, with the assistance of appropriate staff and board members, should be aggressive in the following ways:

- Making certain that the mission statement of the organization is current, compelling, and memorable. It has correctly been observed that mission statements should be no longer than fifteen words.

- Creating and implementing a periodic strategic planning process to determine the organizational direction, and establish priorities and funding needs. The CEO should make certain that the planning activity is not insular, but seeks to involve those persons who, by their knowledge, influence, and wealth, could help bring the vision of the plan to fruition.

- Initiating and being involved in the drafting and approval of an internal case statement based on the strategic plan. The development of the internal case statement enables staff, board members, and essential volunteers to reach consensus on how the organization should be described and builds ownership of its goals.

- Insisting that a thorough communications plan be drafted and approved by the board. The plan should be specific in the objectives to be achieved and the process of accomplishing them.

- Examining the development program budget in light of the organization's funding expectations to make certain that the development staff has the money to do their job.

- Accepting responsibility for working closely with the chief development officer in the identification, cultivation, and solicitation of major gifts.

- Insisting that a complete development action plan for each fiscal year be prepared and approved by the board. The plan should contain the specific objectives, the means to achieve them, and time lines. Included in the plan should be the ways in which the CEO, board members, and other volunteers will be involved in implementing the plan.

THE CEO AND MAJOR GIFTS PROGRAM

There is an old saying in development circles that very few major gifts are consummated without the direct involvement of the CEO. The two big obstacles for CEO involvement are—comfort and commitment.

All CEOs are not automatically comfortable with the role of asking for contributions. Often, they are quite rightly chosen because of their academic credentials, knowledge of the field in which the organization is engaged, management skills, public profile, and the like. Seldom are CEOs chosen because they know how to raise money; yet, this is a usual expectation of the board, whether spoken or unspoken. Some CEO's try to hire a "fundraiser" to take care of this responsibility. This does not work for long or very well. Major donors expect to be courted and asked by the one who represents the organization to them. Board members and other volunteer leadership can open the door, be along on the visit, and help tell the story. But, it is the CEO who must take the lead and, normally, must ask for the gift.

This brings us to commitment. The consummately successful CEO will make a commitment to become knowledgeable in major gifts fundraising and will learn to become comfortable leading this essential part of the development program.

The first step in this process is to ensure that the organization has a major gifts management system that will facilitate the means to acquiring major support. The method that has proven successful in our experience is the MOVES program, originally conceived by Buck Smith. This program assists the CEO, the development director, board members, and volunteers in a purposeful review and categorization of major prospects. Through rating and planning tools, choices are made regarding those prospects who should have a high to lower level of attention, and the first Move is planned.

Since it is recognized that the CEO has more to attend to than major prospects (e.g., managing the organization), he or she is asked to choose a set number of those prospects who are "CEO-level"—or of the highest potential. The number on the list is up to the CEO. However, experience has taught that ten is the outside limit for the head of the organization.

The CEO's head of the development department must become a partner with him or her in managing these prospects. It is recommended that the two meet every other week, at a set time when the CEO's prospects and the planning of MOVES are the only topics. Not only does this keep the proper focus on these major prospects, but the development officer can help the boss become increasingly comfortable and effective in this essential aspect of his/her job.

PROVIDING LEADERSHIP IN STEWARDSHIP

The term "stewardship" is used with great frequency, both in religious and secular society. We tend to take for granted that we and others know what we mean when we use the word, and it is tossed off so that we sound profound without any further exploration of the richness of the concept.

We hear it invoked at least once a year during church annual fund drives, by environmental groups who urge us to take care of planet Earth, by some who encourage us to live frugally so that we can share our leftover resources with others, and by others who equate stewardship with giving time to nonprofit organizations.

Consider our definition of the concept:

Stewardship means taking care of something we value so that we enable it to grow. It calls us to take responsibility and to make a contribution of our whole selves —time, talent, and treasure.

Something we value is a thing we need—that meets our needs. When we inventory those people and organizations that fit this definition, we can begin to understand why we are compelled to help them succeed.

Good leadership, then, requires the chief executive to be intentional about leading the board and staff to commitment and to practice good stewardship in all aspects of their work. The CEO is in a unique position to foster a positive attitude of stewardship. We believe that this emphasis creates a working environment that will be less casual about personal involvement and support.

It is common and wise practice for every nonprofit organization to have an annual financial audit conducted by a nonrelated CPA firm. This, and the publication of an annual report, gives confidence to your staff, board, donors, and the general public that the organization is on sound financial footing and that contributions are being properly used. It gives, as well, insight into your overall financial stewardship.

In addition to the financial audit, we suggest that chief executives conduct a stewardship audit—a personal and organizational review that can help affirm professional and organizational strengths. The audit will also likely identify and remove barriers to fulfilling your mission.

The first step is for the chief executive to evaluate his or her stewardship of staff members.

- Are expectations fair and clear?
- Are the right people in the best positions that utilize their talents?
- Are staff members consulted before making decisions concerning their areas of responsibilities?
- Are you taking the lead in creating an environment that is positive and welcoming?
- Do you encourage a team approach to problem-solving and management?
- Do you give credit and reward quality staff ideas and work?

Next, ask members of your staff to consider their approaches to the organization and their work. As a staff member, each should ask:

- Are you a good steward of your time and the organization's resources?
- Do you look for efficiencies and make your ideas known?
- Do you give extra time and effort, when necessary, to complete a project?
- Do you demonstrate by your attitude your commitment to the organization's mission?
- Do you conduct yourself each day to build better relationships with those with whom you work and with your nonprofit's constituents?

Then, we encourage the chief executive to lead a discussion with the management team. Together, consider the messages that are being used to define your organization, and how you are conveying them to your constituencies.

- Have you defined the key areas/programs that resonate with your prospects and supporters?
- Are these messages being expressed in terms of how your work meets their needs?
- Are there ways, besides giving money, that constituents can be connected to your organization?
- Do you have a clear and compelling statement of the case for support of your organization that includes your commitment to be good stewards of the resources you are given and provide in services to your clients/students?
- Are you being efficient and effective in telling your story through the use of new technologies?

Finally, the chief executive should, in an appropriate time and manner, ask members of the board to discuss their individual commitments to the organization they own and serve. Each member should be encouraged to consider:

- What strengths do you bring to the board that will help move the organization forward?
- Are your strengths being utilized—and if not, will you be proactive in correcting this situation?
- Do you view the budget in terms of how it advances the mission of the organization?
- Do you support the hiring of investment managers based on performance rather than friendship?

- Do you actively find ways to engage more people in knowledge, appreciation, and support for your organization?

- Do you insist on sound stewardship in the management of the organization and support the CEO in these efforts?

- Do you make a financial contribution that is commensurate with your ability and your leadership position?

- Are you providing leadership in planning to set the strategic objectives to ensure the organization has clearly defined its future growth in service?

- Do you insist that each new prospective board member is committed to make your organization a priority?

The practice of good stewardship begins with an appreciation of its importance and continues as a living part of the organization's culture. We recommend that the topic of ways to be better stewards of the organization's resources be a regular item on staff meeting agendas. Further, updates on the subject should be given at every board meeting.

To be a good steward does not mean becoming parsimonious. Instead, stewardship should be viewed as a means to a more abundant and productive organization that is better able to accomplish its goals of service to society.

In Summary

The CEO sets the tone for the public persona and the day-to-day management of the organization. He or she must provide direction for:

- Working with the board to keep all programs and activities within the scope of the organization's mission

- Setting the expectations for the working environment that is welcoming and promotes harmony

- Creating evaluation methods that include the measurement of client and visitor served

- Providing leadership in the marketing and fundraising efforts

- Insuring accurate recordkeeping and reporting of all funds acquired and used by the organization

- Making certain that the wishes of the donor are recorded and respected

- Publishing materials that contain accurate information about the organization's programs and progress

- Practicing the Hippocratic oath of fundraising—*Make no recommendation that would harm the donor or the donor's family in solicitation activities*

- Hiring staff members who bring personal integrity as well as professional skills to the organization

- Being leaders in creating the attitude and the practice of good stewardship for themselves, their staff, and board members.

Most of all, there is no substitute for maintaining high standards and a sense of personal honor as an example to staff as well as the public.

CHAPTER 11

The Development Professional

There are many theories about who will be successful in guiding an organization's program to raise friends and funds. Experience shows us that the best individuals for this calling are those who are more interested in others than in themselves. An author whose name is not known to the writer succinctly describes this fundamental quality of an effective development officer:

> No psychology of dealing with people really works unless we are genuinely and truly interested in other people. All else is trickery and sooner or later will fail.

Successful development professionals honestly like people. Even when tested by those volunteers, prospects, and donors who display unlikeable tendencies, they still look for positive ways to interact with them, and help them have good experiences with the nonprofit they represent.

Development professionals must, in fact, have an optimistic outlook that is deep-seated and real. We are not suggesting that they should be Pollyannaish, but often they are the ones who must believe that fundraising goals will be achieved and who infect and sustain others with that belief.

Those who will be happy and fulfilled in nonprofit marketing and fundraising must be more interested in the organization's success than their own. Self promotion is a sure sign that an individual will not last long in development. If you find yourself wishing you were in the photo with the CEO and volunteers and harbor feelings of resentment because someone else reads and gets credit for copy you have written, you will not likely continue in the profession for very long. By the very nature of the job, the development officer—at every level— works best through the preparation and management of others. Satisfaction is derived from the volunteers' and organization's accomplishments, not whether or not the development staff member gets credit.

In the past, very few people intentionally planned to become a development professional. A number of individuals were busy studying other subjects and pursuing quite different careers when an organization with which they were familiar and in which they were interested presented an opportunity to help them raise friends and funds. In some cases, they were already volunteering for the nonprofit. In other cases, they were on the staff in quite a different role. Whatever their situation, they said "yes" and began a rich professional and personal journey.

The profession is quite different today. Through the efforts of organizations like the Association of Fundraising Professionals, the Council for the Advancement and Support of Education, the publications of scholarly work in the field, and course offerings, including major studies, in a number of universities, individuals are making informed choices about entering the profession. They will be successful if they understand that the profession is more of a calling than a choice.

Why Are Development Professionals Needed?

Now you are wondering why a question has been asked that answers itself—to help lead a nonprofit organization in raising the money it must have to operate, grow, and reach toward fulfilling its mission. We submit that successful development professionals are much more than fundraising functionaries.

Here are some ways that are often overlooked that we believe development professionals serve their organizations:

- Development professionals have been entrusted with the preservation and strengthening of their respective organizations. In this role, they can influence and uphold the proper values of the nonprofit and do so without apology. Since their job is to bring funds to the organization, they have a prominent role to play in keeping the standards high in policies, internal practices, and service delivery, and should not shrink from this responsibility. Development officers can make a positive difference, even in nonprofits that are notably frail but are terribly important to the individuals served and to our society.

- Development professionals must practice—and remind others in their organizations to practice—The "Golden Rule." Who else will write the letter for the CEO to sign thanking an important volunteer? Who, if not the development officer, will make certain that the birthdays and anniversaries of board members, donors, and major prospects are remembered?

- Development professionals should dream of what could be and help keep the vision alive in their CEOs, fellow administrators, faculty, staff, board members, and other volunteers. Funding objectives should not be created in the development office, but there is an important task of making certain organizational vision is not dimmed by day-to-day challenges. After all, people like to give to nonprofits that see what can be and work to reach those plateaus.

- Development professionals should help their CEOs deal with the tremendous pressures that are placed on them. CEOs are too often expected to be "God on a good day." Their development partners should help share the load and keep their bosses motivated.

- Development professionals have value in serving as the consciences of their organizations—to help keep them on track according to their founding principles. Integrity, both for themselves and their nonprofits, cannot be overemphasized. However, this function must not be worn on their sleeves. Then it would be too easy to brush off and too much in view to be believed. Integrity must be integral to development officers—a part of them—the way they are expected and understood to be.

IF DEVELOPMENT PROFESSIONALS ARE SO IMPORTANT, WHY AREN'T THEY APPRECIATED?

A faculty member of a college many years ago was asked by the chief development officer if he would provide a value for a piece of equipment donated to his department by a local industry. He was further asked if he would be a part of expressing thanks to the plant manager for the donation. The faculty member was noticeably disturbed by both requests, finally calling the development officer a "bean counter," and refusing to be a part of of it.

This true story may remind you of encounters you have had with faculty, medical staff, or others who do not consider the process of building relationships and raising funds as important or necessary as the work they are doing. It is easy to feel unappreciated by the unspoken attitudes as well as spoken comments. Do not fall into that attitudinal trap. Instead, if this describes your circumstances, you have an opportunity to build proper relationships with your colleagues. Just as you need an active plan to accomplish your other development objectives, you also need to be intentional about strengthening internal relationships. We recommend one-on-one meetings with departmental chairs, program heads, and some individual staff members to discuss their needs and their joys. You may find that you can help them by researching funding sources to address one or more of their needs and assist in preparing proposals to appropriate foundations and corporations. The more you try to understand them, the better cooperation you will receive from them and the greater will be their appreciation of your work.

That said, you know that you are able to accomplish great things for your nonprofits only to the extent that you work through others. The volunteers you help to achieve will appreciate you; however, it is the volunteer who will receive the praise. Development professionals must get their satisfaction from the promotion of others and accomplishing important organizational goals. In many ways, this requires more strength of character than that of other professions, but the rewards of making certain human needs are met through your efforts is a powerful force. You must resist getting so involved in the minutiae of operating your program that your vision dips and your perspective gets out of alignment.

Development, in our view, is a high calling in that we offer individuals opportunities to invest in improving the human condition. We are the guides for a kind of immortality for donors who become invested in organizations whose missions and services are far greater than any one person.

The Development Chief and the CEO

The attitude of fundraising-reluctance on the part of CEOs was in full display in an article published in *The Chronicle of Philanthropy* about a decade ago. The author reported that nonprofit chief executives were desperately seeking a "professional fundraiser" to head their development programs. If only they could find that super salesperson to solicit major gifts, then they could solve their organizational funding problems. Also, the CEOs reasoned, they could get on with running their organizations without having to be much involved in raising money. We have tried to deal with this in the previous chapter—that chief executives must give leadership to raising major dollars, and they abrogate this responsibility at the peril of their nonprofits. However, a good working relationship between the CEO and chief development officer is essential to securing significant financial support.

A number of years ago, a university president and his vice president for development were faced with a challenge that most nonprofits would welcome. A donor had pledged several million dollars to the university if a like amount could be raised in matching funds. The sum was so significant that success would be transformative, moving the institution from a regional to national presence. The challenge was met, but the methods are more instructive than the amount. This university president and the vice president respected and liked each other. They agreed upon the roles each would play. The president opened his calendar to the vice president so that appointments could be made for him. They met regularly to discuss prospects and strategies and, in the vernacular, "had each other's back."

This is a true story, though it may seem like a fantasy to a majority of development professionals. Yet, when the CEO and the chief development officer establish the proper working relationship, the organizations they serve have the best chance of moving toward fulfilling their missions. Here are a few tips that may help in building the team effort. First, the CEO:

- Should hire a chief development officer that he or she can respect, trust, and enjoy working with
- While not anxious to ask for money, should be open to learning and growing in this critical role
- Should be affirmative about making the development program a high priority in the organization and in the budget
- Should insist on a written annual marketing and fundraising action plan and participate as appropriate in creating strategies
- Should intentionally make time available to the chief development officer for regular planning meetings and for the cultivation and solicitation of major prospects
- Should understand the need to help the chief development officer keep the development team motivated

Next, the chief development officer:

- Should accept the responsibility for creating, with the CEO, the game plan for marketing and fundraising and the responsibility for carrying it out
- Should perform all background work to prepare the CEO for interaction with board members and major prospects and donors
- Should understand the strengths and weaknesses of the CEO and design initiatives that take advantage of his or her talents
- Should always do more than what is expected
- Should understand and accept the role of helping the CEO carry the weight of responsibility for the organization

HOW TO FIND YOUR IDEAL DEVELOPMENT PROFESSIONAL

An organization searching for a chief development officer should carefully consider the qualities described above, carefully define the position and expectations, and set up a procedure that will enable a thoughtful decision. Here is the process we recommend for the nonprofit CEO:

- Begin by appointing a search committee (two or three persons) who will assist you in establishing the process and reviewing/interviewing candidates.
- With the committee, list the qualities and skills that a successful candidate should possess. While the list may change during the search, some qualities may emerge as more important than you initially thought and establish in your mind the kind of person you would feel confident and comfortable working with. This will help you sort through the pile of applicants. Some of these qualities and skills may be:
  - Integrity
  - Personal initiative
  - Sense of timing
  - High self-expectations
  - Well organized
  - Appreciation for your mission
  - Ability to communicate verbally and in writing
- Establish the minimum training and experience that candidates must possess. Consider such areas as:
  - Level of education
  - Years of experience in development
  - Specific fundraising and volunteer management training and experiences
  - Supervision experience
  - Budgeting experience
- Besides the basic requirements you need your candidates to possess, list other desirable qualities and experiences that would be beneficial to your organization, such as proposal-writing skills, experiences with like organizations, and major gift fundraising experience.
- Set up a budget for the search and the salary limit for the position. In addition to the obvious limitations in setting the salary range, there are two other considerations:
  - The current level of your program. Is it at a level of sophistication that the development chief must be an "old hand," or can you hire an eager candidate with the requisite basic skills and enable him or her to grow with your program?
  - The expectations of your chief volunteers. It is important that board members and other key volunteers have confidence in the new development chief.
- Determine how you will build your list of candidates. There are several ways to do this:
  - Advertise locally.

- List the position with the local AFP chapter.
- For a national audience, advertise in the *Chronicle of Philanthropy, CASE Currents*, and other professional publications that target nonprofit practitioners.

- Always post the position internally and take seriously applicants who come from the current staff.

- Make phone calls to other nonprofit professionals to solicit their input.

- Write the interview questions that will be asked of each candidate. Further, write reference questions that correspond to the questions used in the interview. Review these questions with the search committee to get their advice and consent.

- Create with the search committee a time line with specific action steps. This will both help establish what needs to be done and keep the search process moving toward completion.

In Summary

There are many attributes that are desirable in the effective development professional that have been discussed in this chapter. They may be summarized as follows:

- Belief in and commitment to the mission and purpose of the organizations they serve

- Integrity—personal and professional

- Patience, understanding, and enjoyment in dealing with the variety of personalities that come with volunteers

- Determination, creativity, and skills to help volunteers to be successful

- Optimism and motivation to achieve in spite of naysayers who inevitably surround them

- Recognition of the importance of being good stewards of the organization's resources

- Adaptability to rapidly changing situations without allowing those changes to deter the achievement of funding and program goals

- Understanding of the importance of the "Golden Rule" and practicing it—from creating an annual fund piece to thanking a donor or volunteer

- Appreciation of the necessity to take the time to dream about what the organization could be and help to keep the vision alive in the CEO, other staff member, board members, and volunteers

- Comprehension of the need to help share the load of responsibility carried by the CEO. Expectations by boards and constituents place terrific pressures on the chief executive. Some of that pressure will be transferred to the development officer

- Know that they are most productive working through others. They do not expect to be in the limelight; rather, they get satisfaction from the promotion of others and the accomplishment of their organizational goals

We know that we cannot expect perfection, but we have tried to set some standards that will give some specific guidance to those contemplating entering the field and some confirmation to the many who serve our country's rich fabric of nonprofit organizations. Let us conclude by summarizing from the first chapter. Good development officers offer individuals opportunities to invest in human energy and talent, and the chance to help guide succeeding generations. Certainly, they are not "hired guns," but, instead, turn the spotlight on volunteers, the CEO, and board members, rather than on themselves. Successful development officers enable others to achieve their goals, and, in so doing, meet the marketing and fundraising goals of their organizations. For those who understand and accept this role, their lives are enriched by the countless people whose lives have been made better and more productive because of their work. We think it is a wonderful way to earn a living and spend a life.

SAMPLE MONTHLY REPORT — DEVELOPMENT OFFICE

TO: (President/Executive Director/VP/)

FROM: (Development Staff Member)

SUBJECT: Monthly Report _____

Date _____

I. Meetings/Activities
   A. Weekly meetings with President/ED/VP
   B. Met with Development Committee (date)
   C. Gave speech at Rotary Club (date)

II. Calls and Contacts
   A. Total calls/contacts in the month: Face-To-Face
   B. Gift-related calls/contacts (Moves) in the month: _____ Or _____%
   C. Detailed call reports attached for:

        1.
        2.
III. Other
      A. First draft of case statement completed and sent to (name) and board
         development chair
      B. Speakers bureau brochure at the printer—expect completion by
         (date)

CREATING A DEVELOPMENT OFFICE MANUAL

I.   General Comments
     A. Determine what should be included.
     B. Make assignments to each staff member to write/assemble informa-
        tion in specific areas.
     C. Establish a time line for completion.
     D. Review and update annually.

II. Typical Materials Included Are:
     A. Job descriptions of each staff member
     B. Flow charts and description of procedures for receiving, recording,
        and acknowledging contributions of cash, securities, real estate, other
        property, and pledges
     C. Location, type, and content of files; procedures for using files
     D. Telephone operation and answering procedures—who handles what,
        messages, etc.
     E. Basic guidelines for using computer software—accessing records,
        generating mail lists, creating reports, writing and printing letters and
        envelopes, etc.
     F. Samples of each form used by the department, and explanation of
        how and when to use each
     G. Directory of whom to contact for specific information or assistance
     H. Employee benefits, vacation scheduling, personal time, office cover-
        age, holidays, etc.
     I. Development/campaign committee lists with addresses and tele-
        phone numbers
     J. Board of directors with addresses and telephone numbers

DIRECTOR OF DEVELOPMENT SAMPLE JOB DESCRIPTION

The Director of Development is responsible for the planning, supervision and management of activities and projects aimed at building greater public understanding and acceptance and increased philanthropic support of (name of institution)

I. Principal Responsibilities—General

1. Provides assistance in the process of strategic planning
2. Provides advice on internal and external matters that affect the ability of the organization to serve it clients
3. Provides the director and oversees the identification, recruitment, and training of volunteers to serve in advisory, marketing, and fundraising roles
4. Becomes involved in the community in which the organization is located, including membership in a service club
5. Provides counsel to the CEO and chair of the board in identifying potential new board members
6. Prepares and administers the budget for marketing and fundraising.
7. Accepts appropriate special assignments by the CEO

II. Principal Responsibilities—Marketing and Fundraising

1. Responsible for the creation, supervision, and implementation of the annual action plan for marketing and fundraising
2. Responsible for the creation, supervision, and implementation of an organized annual giving program for current operating support
3. Responsible for the creation and direction of an ongoing program to raise major gifts for facilities, equipment, and endowment as approved by the board.
4. Responsible for the creation and direction of an ongoing program to encourage estate-related giving.
5. Responsible for the process of identifying, researching, and recording information on major individual, corporate, and foundation prospects.
6. Responsible for management of the development office.
7. Responsible for providing regular reports to the board on gifts and other departmental activities.
8. Responsible for the program of acknowledging and recognizing gifts
9. Responsible for policies and programs to tell the organization's story to its target markets and to the broader community
10. Responsible for the process of the creation and distribution of all press releases and feature stories

11. Responsible for the supervision of the creation, production and distribution of all internal and external brochures, pamphlets, annual reports, newsletters, and other materials designed to increase public understanding and build stronger relationships with the organization's constituents

12. Responsible for the process of creating all audiovisual materials utilized by staff and volunteers

13. Responsible for creating and implementing evaluation tools to ensure marketing and fundraising efforts are meeting or exceeding objectives

The Director of Development reports directly to the CEO of the organization. In addition, it is expected that he/she will also develop productive relationship with other members of the administrative team, with members of the board, and with other key staff members and volunteers.

About the Author

Brydon M. DeWitt, President of DeWitt & Associates, Inc., has been a development professional for more than 35 years. Mr. DeWitt began his development career in 1973 at Bridgewater College in Bridgewater, Virginia, and served as the chief development officer from 1975–1990. During that period, the College successfully completed two major capital campaigns and significantly increased its annual and major giving programs. In 1990, he accepted the invitation of Gonser Gerber Tinker Stuhr, a development consulting firm in Chicago, Illinois, and began providing counsel to a variety of nonprofit organizations throughout the United States. In 1995, he left the firm to establish DeWitt & Associates, and continued to counsel in fundraising and public relations to a diverse group of clients.

Mr. DeWitt has made presentations and conducted seminars/workshops for conferees and governing boards. Topics have ranged from basic development principles to board development to building effective major gifts programs. The Illinois Hospital Association, American Association of Christian Colleges and Seminaries, AFP of Memphis, Tennessee, and the Virginia Fund Raising Institute have been among the organizations that he has addressed.

He has also taught courses for Virginia Commonwealth University ("Raising Major Funds for Capital Needs" 10/2001 and 5/2002—especially for Nonprofits, Certificate Program) and the University of Richmond ("Building a Powerful Board That Can Raise Money" 11/2001; "Jumpstarting a Stalled Campaign" 2/2002; "Successful Capital Campaign Planning" 4/2002—Office of Community and Professional Education, Institute on Philanthropy). Currently, he is teaching "Nonprofit Marketing, Service-Learning," an elective for VCU senior marketing majors.

In 1996, Mr. DeWitt began writing and publishing *The Development Companion*, a quarterly educational newsletter for presidents, board members, and development officers. Each issue is dedicated to a single topic and provides a step-by-step approach to the operation of a successful development program.

Mr. DeWitt holds a BA degree in English from Bridgewater College, Bridge-water, Virginia, and an MFA in Theatre from Virginia Commonwealth University, Richmond. He is a member of the Association of Fundraising Professionals—Central Virginia, Virginia Association of Fund-Raising Executives, the Virginia Gift Planning Council, and the Rotary Club of Innsbrook. He is past president of the board of directors, Richmond Midnight Basketball League, and continues to serve on the board.

AFP Code of Ethical Principles and Standards

ETHICAL PRINCIPLES • Adopted 1964; amended Sept. 2007

The Association of Fundraising Professionals (AFP) exists to foster the development and growth of fundraising professionals and the profession, to promote high ethical behavior in the fundraising profession and to preserve and enhance philanthropy and volunteerism. Members of AFP are motivated by an inner drive to improve the quality of life through the causes they serve. They serve the ideal of philanthropy, are committed to the preservation and enhancement of volunteerism; and hold stewardship of these concepts as the overriding direction of their professional life. They recognize their responsibility to ensure that needed resources are vigorously and ethically sought and that the intent of the donor is honestly fulfilled. To these ends, AFP members, both individual and business, embrace certain values that they strive to uphold in performing their responsibilities for generating philanthropic support. AFP business members strive to promote and protect the work and mission of their client organizations.

AFP members both individual and business aspire to:

- practice their profession with integrity, honesty, truthfulness and adherence to the absolute obligation to safeguard the public trust
- act according to the highest goals and visions of their organizations, professions, clients and consciences
- put philanthropic mission above personal gain;
- inspire others through their own sense of dedication and high purpose
- improve their professional knowledge and skills, so that their performance will better serve others
- demonstrate concern for the interests and well-being of individuals affected by their actions
- value the privacy, freedom of choice and interests of all those affected by their actions
- foster cultural diversity and pluralistic values and treat all people with dignity and respect
- affirm, through personal giving, a commitment to philanthropy and its role in society
- adhere to the spirit as well as the letter of all applicable laws and regulations
- advocate within their organizations adherence to all applicable laws and regulations
- avoid even the appearance of any criminal offense or professional misconduct
- bring credit to the fundraising profession by their public demeanor
- encourage colleagues to embrace and practice these ethical principles and standards
- be aware of the codes of ethics promulgated by other professional organizations that serve philanthropy

ETHICAL STANDARDS

Furthermore, while striving to act according to the above values, AFP members, both individual and business, agree to abide (and to ensure, to the best of their ability, that all members of their staff abide) by the AFP standards. Violation of the standards may subject the member to disciplinary sanctions, including expulsion, as provided in the AFP Ethics Enforcement Procedures.

MEMBER OBLIGATIONS

1. Members shall not engage in activities that harm the members' organizations, clients or profession.
2. Members shall not engage in activities that conflict with their fiduciary, ethical and legal obligations to their organizations, clients or profession.
3. Members shall effectively disclose all potential and actual conflicts of interest; such disclosure does not preclude or imply ethical impropriety.
4. Members shall not exploit any relationship with a donor, prospect, volunteer, client or employee for the benefit of the members or the members' organizations.
5. Members shall comply with all applicable local, state, provincial and federal civil and criminal laws.
6. Members recognize their individual boundaries of competence and are forthcoming and truthful about their professional experience and qualifications and will represent their achievements accurately and without exaggeration.
7. Members shall present and supply products and/or services honestly and without misrepresentation and will clearly identify the details of those products, such as availability of the products and/or services and other factors that may affect the suitability of the products and/or services for donors, clients or nonprofit organizations.
8. Members shall establish the nature and purpose of any contractual relationship at the outset and will be responsive and available to organizations and their employing organizations before, during and after any sale of materials and/or services. Members will comply with all fair and reasonable obligations created by the contract.

9. Members shall refrain from knowingly infringing the intellectual property rights of other parties at all times. Members shall address and rectify any inadvertent infringement that may occur.
10. Members shall protect the confidentiality of all privileged information relating to the provider/client relationships.
11. Members shall refrain from any activity designed to disparage competitors untruthfully.

SOLICITATION AND USE OF PHILANTHROPIC FUNDS

12. Members shall take care to ensure that all solicitation and communication materials are accurate and correctly reflect their organizations' mission and use of solicited funds.
13. Members shall take care to ensure that donors receive informed, accurate and ethical advice about the value and tax implications of contributions.
14. Members shall take care to ensure that contributions are used in accordance with donors' intentions.
15. Members shall take care to ensure proper stewardship of all revenue sources, including timely reports on the use and management of such funds.
16. Members shall obtain explicit consent by donors before altering the conditions of financial transactions.

PRESENTATION OF INFORMATION

17. Members shall not disclose privileged or confidential information to unauthorized parties.
18. Members shall adhere to the principle that all donor and prospect information created by, or on behalf of, an organization or a client is the property of that organization or client and shall not be transferred or utilized except on behalf of that organization or client.
19. Members shall give donors and clients the opportunity to have their names removed from lists that are sold to, rented to or exchanged with other organizations.
20. Members shall, when stating fundraising results, use accurate and consistent accounting methods that conform to the appropriate guidelines adopted by the American Institute of Certified Public Accountants (AICPA)* for the type of organization involved. (* In countries outside of the United States, comparable authority should be utilized.)

COMPENSATION AND CONTRACTS

21. Members shall not accept compensation or enter into a contract that is based on a percentage of contributions; nor shall members accept finder's fees or contingent fees. Business members must refrain from receiving compensation from third parties derived from products or services for a client without disclosing that third-party compensation to the client (for example, volume rebates from vendors to business members).
22. Members may accept performance-based compensation, such as bonuses, provided such bonuses are in accord with prevailing practices within the members' own organizations and are not based on a percentage of contributions.
23. Members shall neither offer nor accept payments or special considerations for the purpose of influencing the selection of products or services.
24. Members shall not pay finder's fees, commissions or percentage compensation based on contributions, and shall take care to discourage their organizations from making such payments.
25. Any member receiving funds on behalf of a donor or client must meet the legal requirements for the disbursement of those funds. Any interest or income earned on the funds should be fully disclosed.

A Donor Bill of Rights

PHILANTHROPY is based on voluntary action for the common good. It is a tradition of giving and sharing that is primary to the quality of life. To assure that philanthropy merits the respect and trust of the general public, and that donors and prospective donors can have full confidence in the not-for-profit organizations and causes they are asked to support, we declare that all donors have these rights:

I.

To be informed of the organization's mission, of the way the organization intends to use donated resources, and of its capacity to use donations effectively for their intended purposes.

II.

To be informed of the identity of those serving on the organization's governing board, and to expect the board to exercise prudent judgement in its stewardship responsibilities.

III.

To have access to the organization's most recent financial statements.

IV.

To be assured their gifts will be used for the purposes for which they were given.

V.

To receive appropriate acknowledgement and recognition.

VI.

To be assured that information about their donations is handled with respect and with confidentiality to the extent provided by law.

VII.

To expect that all relationships with individuals representing organizations of interest to the donor will be professional in nature.

VIII.

To be informed whether those seeking donations are volunteers, employees of the organization or hired solicitors.

IX.

To have the opportunity for their names to be deleted from mailing lists that an organization may intend to share.

X.

To feel free to ask questions when making a donation and to receive prompt, truthful and forthright answers.

DEVELOPED BY

Association for Healthcare Philanthropy (AHP)
Association of Fundraising Professionals (AFP)
Council for Advancement and Support of Education (CASE)
Giving Institute: Leading Consultants to Non-Profits

ENDORSED BY

(in formation)
Independent Sector
National Catholic Development Conference (NCDC)
National Committee on Planned Giving (NCPG)
Council for Resource Development (CRD)
United Way of America

Index